TRAINING NEEDS ANALYSIS
AND EVALUATION

Roland and **Frances Bee** work as personnel and training consultants in their own business, Time *for* People Ltd, specialising in training needs analysis and training evaluation. They have been involved with a variety of public and private sector clients, mainly in the management training field – in retail, transportation, electronics, the universities and the service sector.

Previously Roland worked as a Chemist with Fisons Fertilisers before serving for 12 years in the RAF as a Navigator. Following this, he worked for 16 years at senior levels in Personnel and Management Services roles in local authorities (seven years as a Chief Officer). During this time he obtained his MA from the Management College, Henley-on-Thames. Subsequently he worked for the London Electricity Board (as Chief O&M Officer) and the Housing Corporation (as Personnel Services Manager).

Frances read Mathematics at Oxford and Statistics at London University. Her early career was in strategic planning at the GLC. On completion of her MBA at Henley she moved into the personnel and training field. She moved into senior management in the financial services area with the Abbey National Building Society. In 1984 she moved into retail with John Lewis Partnership, occupying several senior posts including those of Assistant Finance Director and General Manager of a large department store. In 1990 she joined Roland in the consultancy.

They are co-authors of *Management Information Systems and Statistics*, published by the Institute of Personnel Management in 1990, and *Customer Care* (1995), *Constructive Feedback* (1996), *Project Management* (1997), and *Facilitation Skills* (1998), all published by the Institute of Personnel and Development.

The Institute of Personnel and Development is the leading publisher of books and reports for personnel and training professionals, students, and all those concerned with the effective management and development of people at work. For details of all our titles, please contact the Publishing Department:

tel. 0181-263 3387

fax 0181-263 3850

e-mail publish@ipd.co.uk

The catalogue of all IPD titles can be viewed on the IPD website:

http://www.ipd.co.uk

TRAINING NEEDS ANALYSIS AND EVALUATION

Frances and Roland Bee

INSTITUTE OF PERSONNEL AND DEVELOPMENT

First published in 1994
Reprinted 1995, 1997, 1998

Typesetting by Action Publishing Technology Limited,
Gloucester and printed in Great Britain by
Short Run Press, Exeter

British Library Cataloguing in Publication Data

Bee, Roland
    Training Needs Analysis and Evaluation. –
    (Developing Skills Series)
    I. Title II. Bee, Frances III. Series
    658.312404

    ISBN 0-85292-547-6

The views expressed in this book are the authors' own,
and may not necessarily reflect those of the IPD.

i)

**INSTITUTE OF PERSONNEL
AND DEVELOPMENT**

IPD House, Camp Road, London SW19 4UX
Tel: 0181 971 9000   Fax: 0181 263 3333
Registered office as above. Registered Charity No. 1038333
A company limited by guarantee. Registered in England No. 2931892

Contents

List of figures

List of tables

List of appendices

Introduction

Training needs analysis (TNA) is one of those subjects that often makes the Training Professional wince. There is the feeling that it is important, that they should know something about it and, horror of horrors, perhaps should be doing some of it. But what on earth does it mean? Does it have any relevance outside the textbooks? If so, what is its relevance to the practising Training Professional and how does one set about it? The term training evaluation (TE) often has the same sort of effect − yes, like 'Mother's apple pie', it sounds like a good thing, but does anybody really do it and if so how?

The purpose of this book is to address these issues. It is intended as a very practical book. In it we will try and demystify the whole process of training needs analysis and training evaluation (TNAE) and demonstrate not only their relevance to the workplace, but the vital part both should play in any training activity. However, most important of all we will offer practical advice about how to carry out TNA and how to undertake TE.

Just a brief word on terminology − some writers/practitioners make a distinction between *training* and *development* and there is some debate about what constitutes training. In this book we use the word training in its widest sense. Also, we have used the term *Training Professional* to describe whoever is managing the training − whether as a practising trainer, or as a line manager looking after his or her training responsibilities − in a professional manner.

Training is a major investment − the *Training in Britain* survey (Training Agency, 1989), the latest comprehensive study of training in Britain, estimated that employers spent £18bn on training in 1986/87 and sponsored 145 million training days. A more recent survey (Employment Department, 1993), but limited to medium and large firms and recording only off-the-job training, showed a fall in training activity from 40 million days in 1991 to 26 million days in

1993. This and other surveys tend to indicate that the same number or more people are being trained but the amount of training per employee being trained is falling. Government interventions and encouragement on issues such as National/Scottish Vocational Qualifications (NVQs/SVQs) and Investors in People (IIP) have provided an additional impetus for training. All these factors serve to highlight the importance of ensuring that training is focused — providing the right training for the right people at the right cost. Training needs analysis and training evaluation are vital tools in ensuring that this objective is achieved.

The first key step is to state what we actually mean by the phrases themselves. We define TNA as the whole process of:

- identifying the range and extent of training needs from business needs
- specifying those training needs very precisely
- analysing how best the training needs might be met.

This definition explains the structure of the first four sections of the book and takes us round the first half of what we have called the Training Wheel (see Figure 0.1, page xvi).

Section 1 sets off at the starting point for any training initiative — the business needs of the organisation. We have purposefully called the section Business Needs — The Driving Force. We would argue very strongly that it is the business needs that must drive the training activity and that all training must be clearly linked to identifiable business needs. This section examines the sorts of business needs that can give rise to training interventions.

Next, Section 2, Identifying Training Needs — Translating Business Needs into Action, looks at the link between business needs and performance and how the need for an intervention can be identified. It covers a range of what we will describe as windows into the business needs — the mechanisms that identify the range and extent of the training intervention required. It covers the areas of human resource planning, succession planning, management information systems, critical incidents and appraisal systems. The section ends with the very important chapter asking the question 'Is there (really) a training need?' Very often the knee-jerk reaction to a gap in performance is the magic solution of training. However, in many cases, training will be neither the best nor even an appropriate response and there will be other solutions which will tackle the problem more effectively and possibly more cheaply. The chapter looks at the range of non-training options that might be available.

Section 3, Specifying Training Needs, is about specifying training needs as precisely as possible. Having decided that the performance need is one that would benefit from a training intervention, the next stage is to look at how to specify very precisely the training required. The starting point must be the requirements of the job and, so, the first chapter of this section looks at how to analyse a job to provide the right sort of information required for specifying training. The second chapter looks at ways of investigating the gap between existing performance and required performance.

Having specified the training need, Section 4, Translating Training Needs into Action, then moves on to analyse how this training need can best be met. It looks at the choice of training options available – the formal or informal routes. It describes the vital step of how to prepare a Training Specification – which sets out in detail the requirements for the training. There then follows the key decision of whether to make, ie develop a new course, or buy, ie buy an off-the-shelf course. Or perhaps there is some option that lies between these two. Finally, this section looks at how to set about choosing a training supplier.

Strictly speaking we have now completed the TNA part of the wheel. Section 5, Planning the Training, covers an important part of the process, but one that often gets neglected in the coverage of the training process. It provides help and guidance on putting the information on training needs together, prioritising the training bids, preparing training plans and budgets and monitoring progress.

Our remit for this book does not include training development and delivery and although the Training Wheel shown in full would include this activity, we do not deal with it.

We then move on to Section 6, Evaluating the Training. So what do we mean by evaluation? Some detailed definitions are offered in the introduction to this section, but for now let's stay with the general definition that TE is about measuring the effectiveness of the training. We think it would be fair to say that this is an area where much more can be done and much more should be done than appears to be the case at present. Although we have covered TE in a separate section, the question of how you evaluate your training is not only a vital one but one that should be considered at every stage in the process, from the identification and analysis of training needs, through specification and development, to the delivery of training. This section takes its structure from a model first proposed by Kirkpatrick (1967), looking at four different levels of training evaluation — reaction level, immediate level, intermediate level and ultimate level — so considering training effectiveness from four different perspectives. Two chapters address the key levels of ultimate evaluation, the second of which deals with the difficult but crucial topic of whether, and if so how, you can actually put a monetary value on the effectiveness of your training. The final two chapters deal with the analysis, presentation and use of evaluation results. This section brings us fully around the Training Wheel (see Figure 0.1, page xvi) asking whether in fact the business needs have been met and whether they were met in the most efficient and effective way.

The final section, Section 7, Reflections, looks back on what we have learned about the TNAE part of the training process. It comments on how systematic and effective training will be an essential ingredient to taking organisations forward into a future, which whatever else it is, will be a more competitive one, where quality training will play an increasingly important part and where organisations will have to function at optimum efficiency and effectiveness to survive and grow.

Training is often seen as something that is *done to* people during training courses — people are trained. However, Senge (1990) talks about the learning organisation with the emphasis on the individual learning and where learning becomes a way of life rather than an episodic event. He defines learning organisations as ones:

> where people continually expand their capacity to create the results they truly desire, where new and expansive patterns are nurtured, where collective aspiration is set free, and where people are continually learning how to learn together.

Although this book sets out to be a very practical approach to training needs analysis and evaluation, it is salutary to remember effective training depends on people wanting to learn and change. In all that we do, we need to nurture and encourage that desire and will to learn.

Figure 0.1
The Training Wheel

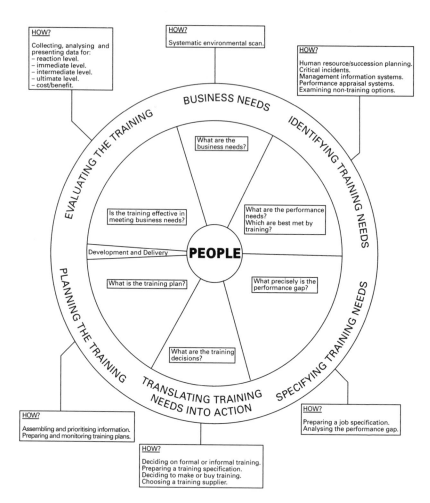

Section 1
Business Needs – The Driving Force

Introduction

It perhaps seems self-evident or, indeed, glaringly obvious that business needs (defined as the operational needs of the organisation whether in the for-profit or not-for-profit sectors) should be the starting point for any training initiative. Boam and Sparrow (1992, p 6) refer to the *strategic triggers* that cause managers to take a look at the skills and competencies of the workforce. However, how many training departments appear to be organised around the preparation and delivery of a catalogue of training courses? In fact, it is only very recently that one newly appointed training manager proudly showed us the culmination of several months' effort − a brochure of training courses which was going to be sent round to managers for them 'to decide which ones they wanted to send their staff on'. This is training activity starting from the wrong end − what the training manager thought might be useful. It is what we call the shotgun approach to training − firing off a a hail of pellets in the hope that one might find the mark, ie meet the need (whatever it is!).

'Hold on one minute', we hear the cry from those for whom this description rings a faint bell, 'this catalogue was compiled after an analysis of what was required'. We would ask how long ago was this analysis carried out? Are the training needs still the same? Who requires training and how do we know which course would be best? To what extent are these courses related to business needs? This is the role of the line manager, some would say, but to what extent have they been trained to carry it out and how much time can they devote to this activity? What a temptation a catalogue of courses presents − all those ready-made solutions to all those difficult performance issues. Which one would seem to fit the bill − 'well this one nearly does, well at least this one will be of some help, or at least it can't do any harm − at least we can say we are trying to do something!'

We would argue that it is this approach to training which

3

has led to the scepticism of senior management that training really is as vital as the Training Professional says it is. Why is it that when things get tough, the training budget is one of the first to face the axe, viewed as a non-productive overhead (Kuraitis, 1981, p 29)? Perhaps one answer is that we have failed to prove that training is essential for an organisation to meet its business goals or that training provides a good return on the investment in it.

Training must be *driven* by the business needs of the organisation. If the link to business needs can be established this will ensure that the training is focused on the real issues and demonstrates its relevance to the business. It also provides the vital starting point for any evaluation of the training.

We believe it is useful to look at the organisation as embedded in its general external environment, (political/ economic, etc) surrounded by its specific external environment, which directly impacts on the achievement of its goals (suppliers, customers, etc), and embracing its internal environment (employees, trade unions, etc). All of these have a stake in the organisation's future. That stake can be a dependent one, eg employee; a combative one, eg competitor; or a collaborative one, eg supplier and/or customer. Chapter 1 looks at the way these environmental factors impact on the business and its needs.

We follow this up in Chapter 2 with an outline of how these factors might drive the business in terms of the planned business needs (the business strategy) and the unplanned business needs (the effects of unexpected and unforeseen events). These business needs then, in turn, drive the various interventions, including training, that an organisation will need to adopt to ensure the success of its business strategy and cope with the buffeting winds of change.

Thus we start on the first part of the journey round our Training Wheel (see Figure 1.1).

Figure 1.1
The Training Wheel — Business needs

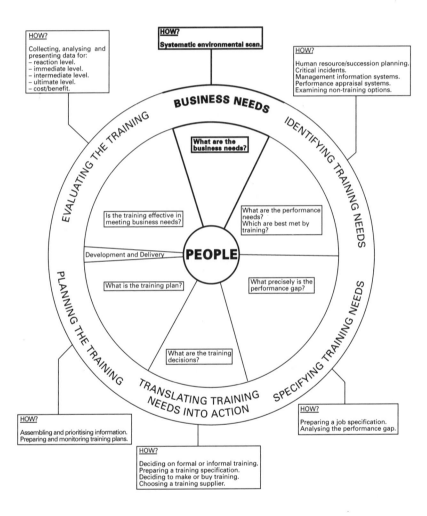

1
Factors Impacting on Business Needs

Introduction

As students of business policy are only too aware, the external environment can pose both major threats and major opportunities to businesses and hence to the Training Professional. The internal environment, or organisational culture, with its attendant strengths and weaknesses can similarly have a significant impact on what strategies businesses are able to adopt to meet those threats and opportunities. It is not intended here to give a comprehensive survey of the impact of these factors on organisations – the reader is referred to a number of good books on business strategy for this (Johnson & Scholes, 1993; Ansoff, 1987; Robbins, 1988). Instead this chapter will look briefly at some of the more common stimuli or triggers prompting changes in business needs. Our list is not meant to be exhaustive but will include:

- general external environmental factors outside the organisation and over which the organisation has no direct control – economic, technological, demographic/social/cultural and political (Robbins, 1988, p 70)
- specific environmental factors over which the organisation might not exercise control but might exert some influence – customers, suppliers, competitors and pressure groups (Robbins, 1988, p 71)
- the internal environment – employees, trade unions and shareholders.

General external environmental factors

Few businesses are not directly affected by the state of the economy, either nationally or locally. Indeed, these days we are well aware that, as a trading nation, Britain is in a global economy and that events on the other side of the world can soon show their effects on our businesses and our lives, whether on interest rates, oil prices or such dramatic changes in markets as the opening up of Eastern Europe and Russia. It is not only the private sector that feels these influences, the not-for-profit sector will be affected as well. Recession and inevitable business closures will mean a reduction in the payment of business rates into the local authority, it will mean a loss of jobs, with a consequent increase in government spending on unemployment and associated benefits. On the other hand, a buoyant economy will mean the reverse – increased confidence of investors with a subsequent growth in business and trading opportunities.

Technology is changing at an ever increasing rate. Today's state-of-the-art computer is tomorrow's junk. Robot assembly plants, laser printers, transplant and genetic surgery – wherever the workplace, whatever the task, there appears to be a technological solution for everything! Technology – whether in the military (with laser-guided weapons), the universities (with tutorials in different countries linked by satellite), the retail sector (with sales-based ordering systems) – is here to give the competitive edge to whoever can use (or afford) it. Changes in technology, with their impact on the numbers and skills of the workforce, pose a major challenge for most organisations and those responsible for the human resources of those organisations. One sure thing is that changing technology will mean shortages in those particular skill-based areas. The non-training solution is to recruit/poach them from elsewhere – but from where? They never seem to exist in the numbers required, training may be the only solution in this case.

Demographic, social and cultural changes are potentially an area of major impact for most organisations, either through the implications for the staffing of the business or for the demands for their products and services. Demographic changes in the UK, such as a potential shortage of school leavers in the 1990s, may have serious implications for future recruitment and result in the need for alternative strategies such as attracting women returners and the greater use of older employees. The growth in women's expectations of their work role and the increased incidence of divorce and one-parent families have led to a substantial increase in the number of women in the labour force. Other social changes, such as a greater proportion of people entering higher education and the influence and needs of ethnic minorities will have their effect too, as well as the more business-related social and cultural changes such as the move towards the learning organisation. Demands for products and services are affected by such demographic changes as the ageing population, with its different needs and expectations, and such social changes as the increased time for leisure and growing concern for the environment. All of these potentially could lead to some sort of training intervention.

Changing legislation, too, has resulted in major and on-going training initiatives. We are now increasingly seeing the impact of legislation resulting from our membership of the European Union. Depending on the nature of the business it can be a major stimulus for action which can often involve training of some sort. Good examples of this has been the legislation on data protection, health and safety, and legislation affecting specific groups such as transport workers (Transport and Works Act 1992). Government can also have an influence other than through legislation, through initiatives such as NVQs/SVQs and IIP.

Specific environmental factors

One of the factors that has a major impact on a business is its customers. To ensure that they hold on to customers in today's intensely competitive markets many organisations make significant strategic moves to satisfy their customers' requirements. Quality initiatives and customer care programmes are good examples.

Suppliers, ie those people or organisations from whom a business obtains its equipment, raw materials and/or services, can have a big impact on that business as well. The stability, timing and the costs of supplied goods and services can play a critical part in the success of a business. The importance of the relationship between supplier and supplied advocated by the Japanese has been highlighted by initiatives to build strong collaborative links, such as developing common working practices and joint training schemes.

No organisation, even those in a virtual monopolistic position, can afford to ignore the competition. Perhaps the classic historical example of this sin was the British motorcycle industry. Previously pre-eminent on the roads of the world until the Japanese motorcycle came from nowhere to knock it into oblivion. What the competition is doing or not doing will provide a major stimulus for action in most organisations.

The latter part of the 20th century has seen growth in the pressure group phenomenon. These range from highly organised and vocal groups such as Friends of the Earth with their campaigns to protect the environment and the animal protection groups with their concerns about the use and exploitation of animals, to *ad hoc* groups which are set up, say, to oppose the building of a bypass or new superstore, at least 'not in my backyard'. Organisations have had to become increasingly aware and sensitive to these types of pressure and have had to learn how to respond appropriately.

Internal factors

Another major stimulus to business needs comes from the necessity for the human resources of the business (eg managers, support staff, shop-floor workers, peripheral and core workers, contractors and consultants) to be kept up to date in expertise, to be motivated and focused on the business objectives. The pressures to be well managed, fairly rewarded for what they do and developed to their full potential come from all categories of staff. The strategic plan that does not take into account the needs for and of their workforce is a plan that is doomed to failure. We will demonstrate in Chapter 3 the value to the organisation of a well-conceived and executed human resource plan as an integral part of the corporate plan.

Another factor that can have a significant impact on the success of the business is the relationship between organisations and their employees that is often represented by the trade unions or their equivalents. In the 1970s, the power of the trade unions appeared to be a major pressure on organisations in Britain. Their seemingly endless desire to enter into strike action led elsewhere in the world to the description of industrial unrest as the British disease. It seems now that enormous growth in management training at the time did little to help cope with this particular pressure on business. Could it be that it was not focused on the real training need? Although the power of the trade unions is much less in the 1990s than it was in the 1970s there is little doubt that the relationship between organisations and their employees, through their trade unions where appropriate, is an important strategic factor and one where there could be a substantial competitive edge for getting it right.

The influence, too, of shareholders on businesses can be very great. It can range from the financial effects on a business's strategy of providing an adequate/growing level of dividend through to influencing the whole policy and direction of the business. The growth of employee shareholders has added another dimension to their role. Very few businesses can afford to ignore the needs and views of their shareholders.

Conclusion

The effects of this range of external and internal factors on business needs for some organisations have been dramatic. Some have retracted to a small range of specialist products, others have diversified. Some have been able to disperse their operations, others have centralised on their core workers (Handy, 1989). Some have failed, others have survived and grown. The next chapter goes on to look at how these factors impact on the development of business strategy, and the ability of organisations to cope with unforeseen and unplanned events.

2
Planned and Unplanned Business Needs

Introduction

All organisations are subject to continuous stimuli for action. At one end of the spectrum is the proactive, planned pressure of the business strategy. At the other end is the knee-jerk reaction to unforeseen and unexpected pressures. In response to the planned pressures – internal and external – many organisations these days have mission statements, goals and objectives and some plan of how to achieve them within both long-term and short-term horizons. These strategies in summary may be for:

● consolidation, ie strengthening the current position but essentially staying the same
● growth via:
  – market penetration, ie increasing the market for existing products
  – market development, ie moving into new markets
  – product development, ie developing new products
  – diversification – related, ie in some way related to the existing business such as moving up or down the supply chain, or unrelated, ie into completely new areas of business
● contraction, ie reducing activities, via:
  – withdrawing from markets
  – withdrawing products
  – selling off/closing down parts of the business
● closure, ie closing the whole business.

The implications of these strategies can be enormous for the human resource side of the business and in particular for the Training Professional. We will take a look at each of these in turn and then at the effects of the unplanned business needs.

⚜ Consolidation

Strengthening the existing business can be a major strategy in its own right. We have shown in Chapter 1 how the continuous changes in the external environment mean that no organisation can afford to stand still but must continuously strive for higher levels of performance. This can be in terms of greater productivity, increased efficiency and inevitably higher quality of goods and services. Aiming to achieve these goals puts greater pressure on the employees of the organisation. How do you achieve higher productivity, increased efficiency and higher levels of quality? What interventions do you need to make? Each of these requirements could provide the starting point for a *needs analysis*, which *might* result in a training intervention, eg training for new processes or procedures to speed up the work flow, or training in customer care.

Growth and diversification

This strategy opens up a potential Pandora's box of interventions. Increased market penetration could pose extra demands on the sales and marketing personnel and the distribution function. Moving into new markets may require the acquisition of new sets of skills, eg languages if moving into new geographical areas, knowledge of clients' businesses and needs if moving into new sections of a market. Moving into completely new business areas can pose even greater demands on employees than straightforward growth as it can imply the need to learn about the whole range of new products, new markets, new technologies, new legislation, etc. The training implications of these strategies can be enormous and require detailed analysis and planning. It highlights the need for the Training Professional to be involved at the earliest possible stages in the planning process. Very often they are involved after the decisions have been taken — how much better for the organisation if they were involved in the strategy-making process itself!

Contraction and closure

Sadly, more of us in the 1980s and 1990s have experienced the pressures associated with cutback and closure than we have experienced the joys of growth. The strategy of decline can result in a surprising and sometimes unexpected amount of training need. With contraction, the remaining employees may be required to take on additional and different work and responsibilities. This may result in the need for multi-skilling, enhanced management skills, etc. Contraction may go hand-in-hand with a radical review of the whole business to ensure that the organisation is on a stronger base for moving forward at a later date. The review may result in the need for major changes in work practice and often in the under-lying culture and attitudes with attendant requirements for training.

Most employers these days take an enlightened view on trying to ease the path of those employees that are being required to leave the business. The provision of training in job-seeking skills often forms part of a severance package. Similarly for those taking early retirement, the provision of courses − ranging from financial management to developing new interests − are becoming almost the norm.

Unplanned business needs

We have talked so far about the business and training needs arising from some form of planned action by the business. At the other end of the spectrum are the business needs arising from the myriad of unforeseen events that can buffet a business. These can range from *minor* operational problems with, for example, a part of the distribution system, faults in the computer system, a flurry of customer complaints to *major* problems such as the failure of a major advertising campaign, or a serious defect occurring with a product or the loss of a major customer. The characteristics of this sort of business need is that it arises usually with the label − super urgent, somebody do something quickly − attached to it. Training often appears to fit the *do something quickly* bill

13

rather well. Ill-conceived, poorly thought through, training is often thrown at the problem before it is even established exactly what the problem is. What are the customer complaints about? What is/are the real cause(s) of the problems? Do they affect all products/services or only some? Do they affect all staff or only some? Is it a *people* problem at all?

It is essential as Training Professionals to try and avoid being catapulted into providing instant solutions which so often can be costly and, worst of all, ineffective. Analysing the exact nature of the problem may take time at the beginning but will ensure that the solution provided will actually do the trick. The chapter on Critical Incidents (Chapter 5) discusses these issues and uses case studies to show how these problems can be approached.

Alternatively it can be an equally difficult and frustrating problem for the Training Professional not to be involved at all in the solution of these business crises. It highlights the need for the Training Professional and training itself to be seen as a key part of the operation of the business and not just as an overhead. The only way this will occur is if training is approached in just the same way as any other intervention/ activity to improve the business − as cost-effective solutions to clearly identified business problems.

It also requires the Training Professionals to develop methods of keeping themselves informed about what is going on in the organisation − systems of environmental scanning (Robinson & Robinson, 1989), and developing their strategic awareness (Sloman, 1994). These methods can be formal − such as sitting on committees, being involved in project/ focus teams, making sure that they are on the circulation lists of key reports, monitoring the relevant internal statistics, etc. Additionally, and sometimes equally useful, are the informal approaches − having coffee/lunch with a wide range of managers in the business, talking to delegates on training courses about their work − what business challenges and problems they are facing, etc.

Training Professionals must scan their external environment in exactly the same way as they scan the internal environment. The mechanisms for so doing will be the same in large part and good internal scanning will also pick up many of these external stimuli. Activities such as attending conferences and seminars, in addition to reading the personnel, training and relevant trade journals, will all help with this process. Above all, it involves showing an interest in the business in the widest sense and showing an understanding and vision of the key issues affecting the business.

Conclusion

This chapter has recognised that we live in an uncertain and dynamic world. Our ten-year/five-year, through to one-week plans, may come to nothing in the face of the organisation responding to the multitude of pressures on it. Managing rapid change, be it through consolidation, growth, contradiction and/or closure, will be the stock-in-trade of managers in the future. As Training Professionals, we need to recognise this and be able to work with it.

We chose as the title for this section Business Needs – The Driving Force because we see the business needs of organisations as not just the starting point for any TNA, but the force that should be driving the training. Training Professionals who fail to understand this perhaps should not be too surprised when their line manager colleagues fail to support them.

How does this all affect the Training Professional? The word that springs to mind is *opportunity*. Change, of whatever nature, arising from planned or unplanned business needs is a golden opportunity for the Training Professional to get involved. So the messages are:

- get your environmental scans going
- make sure you are at the forefront of the organisation in knowing both what is going on now and what changes are on the horizon.

In the next section we look at how these business needs might be translated into action that, where appropriate, will lead to a training solution.

15

Section 2
Identifying Training Needs –
Translating Business Needs into Action

Introduction

In the Introduction to the book we defined TNA as the process encompassing the three stages of:

- identifying the range and extent of training needs from the business needs
- specifying those training needs very precisely
- analysing how best the training needs might be met.

In the first section we began at the top of the Training Wheel with the business needs. This section discusses those techniques which could be called the principal tools of the next stage of the process − which translate the business needs into the need for action to improve or add to the performance of the human resource asset of the business. That action may or may not lead to a training intervention. So this stage in itself can be seen as having two parts:

- identifying the need for the improvement in perfomance or addition to the competencies of the business's staff
- identifying which of these needs require a training intervention.

We will look first at five main tools or, perhaps, what are better described as windows that help us look into the business needs of the organisation. These are:

- human resource planning
- succession planning
- critical incidents
- management information systems
- performance appraisal systems.

The section is structured under these headings, with the final chapter addressing the specific question of whether training is the appropriate intervention to meet the business needs. Many people see succession planning as a subset of human resource planning, but we have chosen to cover it separately as it offers such a fertile source of information on possible training needs.

Traditionally, many books on TNA (Stewart & Stewart, 1978; Goldstein, 1986; Kubr & Prokopenko, 1989) have set out to look at the different *levels* at which training needs are assessed. Some writers use these as levels which indicate the extent of the training and others use them as ways to classify methods for identifying training needs. The most common structure of levels is as follows:

- the organisational level − identifying training needs which affect the whole organisation, eg training aimed at introducing cultural change across the organisation or induction training (also used to indicate assessment to identify where in the organisation training is required)
- the occupational/group level − identifying training needs which affect particular occupations or groups, eg training in new accounting procedures for the finance staff, on new hygiene legislation for catering staff
- the individual level − identifying training needs of individuals, eg a particular member of staff requiring time management training, or the skills to operate a new piece of machinery.

Most writers recognise that they do not form clear and distinct divisions but are interconnected and overlap. It is not our intention to use these levels as a method of structuring, but we will refer to them as and when we feel it is helpful to use this sort of classification.

Another distinction that is sometimes used (Boydell, 1990; Kubr & Prokopenko, 1989) is whether training is for present or for future needs. Again in very general terms:

- present needs are seen to relate current objectives, eg training in competencies required for a current job or to deal with some immediate changes in the environment
- future needs relate to long(er) term objectives, eg training for some future job, to deal with some future planned

change of direction for the business or long(er) term change in the environment.

In our view the distinction has its relevance in helping prioritise and plan the timing of training. Clearly present needs will often seem more pressing than future needs. However, the Training Professional has to be careful to avoid the temptation to concentrate on the present at the expense of the future. Our view is that the rigid separation of training into present and future needs can sometimes get in the way of the overall approach to the identification of training needs and again we shall restrict ourselves to commenting on the distinction as and when it seems helpful.

There is no one best approach to identifying performance/training needs in a systematic way. There is no algorithm or simple flow chart that can be followed by rote. Training Professionals need to be aware of all the sources of information or windows into the business needs. They need to be continuously scanning their business environment with the following questions always in the forefront of their minds:

- first, what performance changes are needed to meet the business needs?
- and second, can those performance changes best be met by a training intervention?

We go on now to examine these windows into the business needs, starting with a look at human resource planning, but first we take a look at our Training Wheel in Figure 2.1 to see how identifying training needs fits into the overall picture.

Figure 2.1

The Training Wheel – Identifying training needs

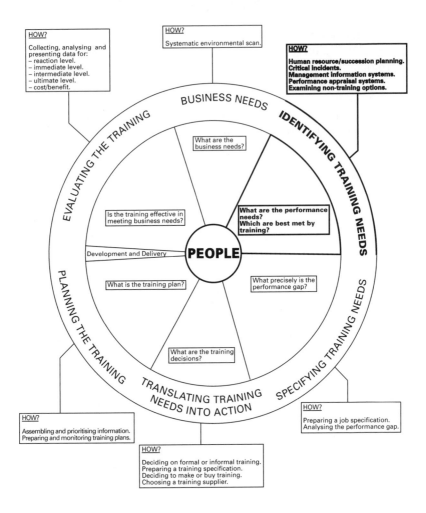

3

Human Resource Planning

Introduction

Boydell (1990, p 16) describes human resource plans succinctly as being:

> To ensure adequate numbers of competent personnel in particular occupations, at given times, consistent with, and related to, the overall business strategy.

So, the starting point for the human resource planning process is, not surprisingly, that the business strategy and human resource plans provide a very potent source of information, or a very effective window, into the business needs for the subsequent identification of training needs. Armstrong (1991, p 289) sets out the aims of human resource planning as being, among other things, to ensure that the organisation:

- obtains and retains the quantity and quality of people it needs
- can develop a well-trained and flexible workforce, thus contributing to the organisation's ability to adapt to an uncertain and changing environment.

The calculations of the quantity and quality can range from a fairly simple comparison of demand for labour against supply over a short period for a small business through to a process for large organisations involving sophisticated and complex computer models looking as far ahead as 10 or 20 years. It can be considered as formal in the sense of a detailed written plan, or informal, covering the planning related to the change in manpower resources required by a new policy statement such as an emphasis on customer care or a move into a new market area.

The purpose of this chapter is not to explain how to do this planning but to explain how human resource plans can be used as a very powerful means of identifying performance change/training needs in order to help develop a well-trained workforce. It is essentially concerned with identifying needs at the organisational and occupational levels and as the name suggests is directed towards future needs. We will use two simple case studies to illustrate how human resource plans can be used to aid the Training Professional in this.

Case study 1 The Rationalisation Company

For competitive business reasons the Rationalisation Company plans to reduce employee numbers, cutting out some levels of management and merging certain functions. The existing staffing levels and the forecast for required staffing in the next year are as set out in Table 2.1. What are the implications for required performance changes and possible training needs?

Let us look first of all at what is happening in global numbers terms. The total numbers employed are planned to decrease by just over 26 per cent, from 944 employees down to 698 employees.

At first sight, the Finance Director suggests cutting the training budget by at least 26 per cent. Seems logical, or does it? Let's look at the figures more closely? Table 2.2 analyses the changes by the groupings of staff.

The big impact is in supervisory and management grades, with reductions in numbers of 58 per cent and 43 per cent respectively. Looking at the supervisory grades first, the ratio of supervisors to unskilled staff has halved, from a ratio of 1:3 (169:507) to 1:6 (71:431). This could be described as a doubling of the supervisory workload and what is more there could be substantial differences in the actual role of the supervisor when managing teams of about six compared to teams of about three. Also, with the merger of two departments, production and distribution, this could mean that the supervisors are managing mixed teams from both areas. Your antennae should be well and truly buzzing − there is likely to be the need for substantial performance changes from the supervisors. A similar picture is likely to emerge for the management grades as well.

24

Table 2.1

Staffing by department

Present staffing			Future staffing		
Finance:	Management	25	Finance:	Management	15
	Technical	30		Technical	30
	Admin/clerical	40		Admin/clerical	30
Sales:	Management	16	Sales:	Management	10
	Technical	29		Technical	30
	Admin/clerical	36		Admin/clerical	20
Production:	Management	16	Production:	Management	13
	Technical	24			
	Admin/clerical	14			
	Supervisory	130			
	Unskilled	380			
Distribution:	Management	10	Distribution:	Technical	38
	Technical	24		Admin/clerical	10
	Admin/clerical	4		Supervisory	71
	Supervisory	39		Unskilled	431
	Unskilled	127			
TOTAL		944	TOTAL		698

Table 2.2

Staff change analysis

	Present (No)	Future (No)	Change (%)
Management	67	38	− 43
Technical	97	98	+ 1
Administrative/clerical	94	60	− 36
Supervisory	169	71	− 58
Unskilled	507	431	− 15

Let's take a look now at the administrative and clerical staff − a reduction of 36 per cent. So, what is happening to their workload? It is just possible with the overall cutback of

26 per cent there might be a reduction of admin/clerical work of about the same order, but the reduction in staff is even greater than this. It could well mean that the remaining staff are going to have to cover wider areas of work, and perhaps the reductions will involve the introduction of new technology and procedures. Do you see the need for some sort of performance changes? Almost certainly!

The reductions plus the merger suggest a lot of change. How is it going to be introduced? Will managers and supervisors need new skills to cope with this level of change? What about the staff that are leaving, is the business going to offer help to ease the move, such as improving job-seeking skills?

The Finance Director is not looking so cheerful now. However, training may not be the only or best intervention to achieve these performance changes. The new demands on the managers/supervisors could be met by recruiting appropriately skilled and trained managers/supervisors or perhaps the business will hire consultants to implement the changes. However, it is a fair bet that training will feature quite large. Far from cutting back on the training budget, the Training Professional may well be looking for an increase next year!

Clearly more information and analysis is required to identify precisely the performance changes required and the appropriate solutions. However, the Training Professional's scan of the environment, in this case the human resource plan, has put him/herself in the position of being ahead of the game, of being in the position to be proactive towards meeting the business's needs. Using the plan as a diagnostic tool, the Training Professional is no longer just reacting to other people's interpretation of the business needs and, therefore, probably at too late a date for the training intervention to be planned and implemented in the most effective way.

Let's move on to another example now aimed at the occupational level. This time where there is no ready supply of the skills required from outside so the recruitment solution is not an option and new staff have to be trained by the organisation.

Case study 2 The Expanding Railway Company

The business plan for the Expanding Railway Company has indicated an ambitious expansion of services and it is recognised that a key human resource requirement for this expansion is train drivers. An additional factor that has put the spotlight onto the train drivers is that it is such a specialist skill that the only reliable source is from drivers coming from the company's own driver training school.

The information that has been fed into the assessment is as follows:

- the starting point is the existing establishment of 200 drivers
- the extra drivers required over the next five years due to new lines being opened is: Year 1, 0%; Year 2, +25%; Year 3, +30%; Year 4, +33.3%; Year 5, 0% (these figures refer to the end of the year and indicate year-on-year percentage changes)
- the crude index of labour turnover forecast is: Year 1, 10%; Year 2, 20%; Year 3, 20%; Year 4, 20%; Year 5, 10%.
- a wastage rate of 10% is forecast for new recruits failing training during the year.

What are the implications of this manpower plan?

The obvious starting point in the analysis is to produce a schedule of the flow of drivers into the organisation over the five years. It might look something like Table 2.3.

What do these figures tell us about the training need? Well, the first and most obvious nugget of information is that there will be approximately a fivefold increase in training need in Year 2. Then after only a slight increase in Year 3, it will more than double in Year 4, before being substantially reduced in Year 5!

The main implications are these:

- Substantially more driver instructors will be needed in Year 2 and again in Year 4. Where will they come from?

27

Table 2.3

Driver recruitment

	Year				
	1	2	3	4	5
Numbers of drivers needed at the start of the year	200	200	250	330	440
Increase due to business needs	0	50	80	110	0
Numbers of drivers needed at the end of the year	200	250	330	440	440
Labour turnover (based on % of average yearly figure)	20	45	58	77	44
Numbers available at the end of the year if no action taken to recruit	180	155	192	253	396
Deficit	20	95	138	187	44
Trainee failures	2	10	14	19	4
Total trainees recruited	22	105	152	206	48

Will they be a further drain on the existing driver pool, requiring a further recruitment of trainees? What training will they require?

- What additional facilities will be required, such as training accommodation, specialist simulation equipment, etc?
- The figures may also give an indication of the need to extend administrative and clerical support for the training function, with the attendant training of these employees in their duties.
- Finally, the decrease in Year 5 needs to be planned. What is to happen to the surplus instructors? It could indicate some redundancies among the instructors and others if no steps are taken to redeploy them into the workforce.

There could also be some surplus training accommodation for use on other programmes.

The essential points to come out of this exercise on drivers is that it enables the Training Professional to plan ahead for a key performance need, in this case toward the strategic decision for expansion, requiring additional employees with driving skills. The meeting of the driver targets is almost certainly crucial to the success of the business plan. In planning well ahead it will increase the probability that these targets will be met and what is more, in the most cost-effective way. It it also identifies a secondary level of performance need, for trained driver instructors. It highlights the need to look at some sort of career management route for driver instructors, perhaps seeing a period of secondment into training as the beginning of some future move into a management/supervisory role.

The computer has a lot to offer in terms of the number crunching required in human resource planning. There is a wide range of systems that have the capacity to calculate changes in numbers and types of staff from changes in business output levels. The associated model of the business allows us to play our what if games – ie if we increase (decrease) turnover by X per cent, what are the staffing implications? Once we know the staffing changes arising from the business changes we are well on the way to identifying the performance needs and hence the training need.

Conclusion

Human resource planning can be as sophisticated or as simple as we want to make it. However, it offers a golden opportunity for the Training Professional to:

- work directly towards the organisation's strategic decisions
- be in the vanguard of the organisation's move into the future.

We next turn our attention to the specific area of succession planning, which is another very useful source of information for the Training Professional.

4

Succession Planning

Introduction

In the last chapter we discussed what a powerful tool overall human resource planning can be in the identification of performance needs and hence training needs. We turn now to a particular form of human resource planning, succession planning. As with human resource plans, succession plans are rooted in the business strategy for the organisation and provide a powerful link between the business needs and the needs for performance changes/training needs. Again our intention is not to explain how to do succession planning but to comment on its implications for identification of performance/training needs. After providing some definitions we use a case study as a vehicle for demonstrating the use of succession plans as a window into the business needs.

Armstrong (1991, p 479) explains that the aim of succession planning:

> is to ensure that, as far as possible, suitable managers are available to fill vacancies created by promotion, retirement, death, leaving or transfer. It also aims to ensure that a cadre of managers is available to fill the new appointments that may be established in the future.

The first part of this definition is quite straightforward but the second part is very dynamic. It implies that succession planning is not simply about replacing existing managers but is about gazing into the crystal ball to determine what management skills in what quantities are required in the future. This is no mean task and the implications for identifying performance/training needs are potentially very considerable. Wallum (1993, p 43) develops this view beyond the manager role and into what he calls key, future roles by stating that succession planning, to be really effective, should encompass:

the strategic process and actions aimed at ensuring a suitable supply of suitable successors for senior or key jobs and future roles.

This definition highlights the significance of succession planning for the identification of performance/training needs. Here we are dealing with the key human resources of the business where failure to deliver the goods will almost certainly have a significant impact on business performance.

Succession planning can be used at the organisational and the occupational levels but is more likely to be used in defining individual needs, particularly for management staff. Succession planning is to do with future needs but covers the range from the near future (simply filling the vacancies caused by labour turnover) to the far distant future (the strategic process). Here again is the opportunity for the Training Professional to be involved in the strategic decisions of the business.

Let us look at a case study to see how these principles can be brought out.

Case study 3 The Planahead Organisation

Succession plans usually take as their starting point the organisation chart. This is then annotated to show the key information required for succession planning. Figure 2.2 shows the succession plan for the management tiers of the Planahead Organisation over a five-year period.

Names of jobholders appear underneath the job titles, as on the organisation chart, with the additional information of their age and the period of time they are expected to be in post (in brackets), where known. For example, J Soap is the managing director, she is 55 years of age and has made it clear that she will retire at age 60. The deputy MD has no name attached, indicating that this is a new post that is expected to be introduced within the next year.

The other names, in the offset boxes, are those of the heirs apparent, or at least those members of staff believed capable of meeting the demands of the senior jobs at some stage in the future.

Figure 2.2
The Planahead Organisation – Management succession plan
Management Succession Plan 1996–2000

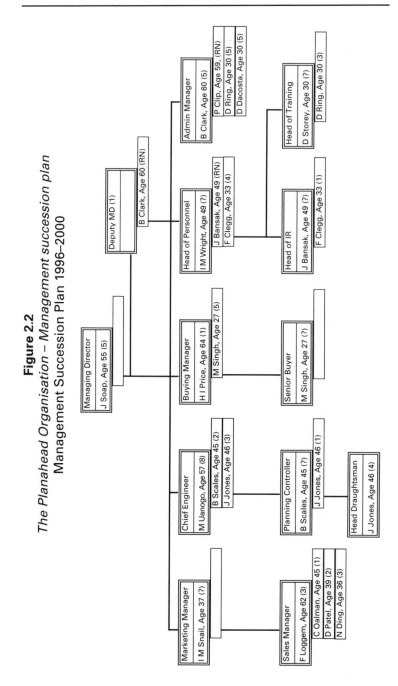

Their ages are given and the period of time before they are expected, in the normal course of events, to have the full set of competencies for the senior posts, ie they are ready to assume the full duties and responsibilities (in brackets). 'RN' means they are ready now. If no other names are given, no one, as yet, has been identified as a possible successor for the job.

The period of time needed to acquire the full competencies for the key jobs shown assumes that some form of formal training or experiential learning is in place to provide the skills and knowledge needed. This, in turn, implies that some form of training needs analysis has been carried out already to identify the training required to prepare those individuals for their future posts. Often this has not been done in any systematic way and this provides the first potential area for intervention for the Training Professional.

The next stage is to look at the overall succession plan for gaps and weaknesses. On the basis that it might be prudent to have more than one successor for each key or senior post, the immediate response to examining the chart shows that some posts (Sales Manager, Head of Personnel) are more than adequately covered, others are covered by only one possible successor, and some (Marketing Manager, Senior Buyer and Head Draughtsman) have no cover at all. However, this is not the only problem thrown up by the chart, other possible problems for the Planahead Organisation are:

- The Buying Manager is due to retire in one year but his possible successor will not be ready for five years.
- In addition to having no nominated successor, the career intentions of the Marketing Manager are not known. If she leaves in the short term, the organisation would appear to be committed to external recruitment.
- The possible candidate for the new Deputy Managing Director is the administration manager but if the Deputy MD job is seen as staging post for filling the MD post, is it sensible to appoint someone who will retire at about the same time as the MD is due to leave?

At this stage it is important to focus on all possible solutions to these problems – the Training Professional is looking initially for how the *performance needs* implied by the succession plan can be met. Training may or may not provide the answers. Let's look at one or two of these problems in more detail:

- In the cases of the Head Draughtsman and Senior Buyer, for whom there are no successors identified, perhaps the next vacancy that arises in their sections should be filled by someone with supervisory experience or training in order to provide a potential heir. In other words, the personnel specification for filling such vacancies should be modified to include some competency in supervision or managerial skills.
- So far as cover for the Marketing Manager is concerned, perhaps one way of postponing the problem is to secure some knowledge about Snail's plans. If you look at the age profile of the top managers you will see that Snail is considerably younger than her colleagues. Snail is clearly a high flyer and might be encouraged to make a commitment to remaining with the organisation by the prospect of being groomed as a possible candidate for the new Deputy Managing Director role. Another approach might be to expand her role and give her wider responsibilities than marketing − possibly, say, by combining marketing with buying when Price retires.

If some of the solutions suggested above are not acceptable either to management or to the employees concerned the Training Professional needs to look wider afield. For example, if the combination of marketing with buying does not secure the longer term commitment of the marketing manager or if I M Snail looks like getting the Deputy MD post in a year's time, then there is a need to pencil in a possible successor. A little creative thinking might be helpful − the Training Professional needs to ask what are the competencies that managers need at the most senior levels in organisations. Perhaps vision and strategy are more important than professional knowledge and skills. While it might be traditional in, say, engineering to have an engineer in the top job it is open to us to ask the questions:

35

- To what extent is senior management about motivating and leading people, about planning and organising, and about dealing with budgets?
- To what extent is the role of top managers about administering their function?

If the answers to either of these questions is larger than modest then you might start to look at how you could groom, say, the Head of Personnel to at least cover on a temporary basis for the Marketing Manager should she be appointed as the new Deputy MD or decide to leave before a true successor is ready. The following options might be considered:

- Train the Head of Personnel in the full range of marketing competencies − tempting but probably impractical on a number of points such as cost and length of time taken.
- Give the Head of Personnel some introductory overview of the marketing function if this is lacking and also arrange for him to get involved in the marketing department/ function at every opportunity, eg recruitment of marketing staff, any disciplinary or performance issues, or even training needs analysis in the department. In these ways the Head of Personnel could quickly gain some competence in the issues facing the function, to add to the senior management skills already gained through working at the top level.

So far we have looked at the obvious business need of the organisation of ensuring that it has suitable successors to its key management posts. Another set of problems that might be identified by the eagle-eyed Training Professional is what to do with those staff that are ready for promotion now or within the next year and where there is no opportunity for this promotion in the short term. For example, there is C Oalman who is shown as a successor for the Sales Manager, F Loggem, who is not due to retire for another three years and J Bansak, if the Head of Personnel does not move on. There is the danger of such staff becoming demotivated, with the consequent negative impact on their work and on the motivation of those around them, or the possibility of them leaving. Solutions that may help to bridge the gap are second-ments to gain wider experience of the organisation, joining project teams to hone up project management skills or under-taking some additional professional or general management training.

So, as you can see, the succession plan can provide a rich source of information on performance and training needs. It is often said, with some justification, that the Training Professionals are left out of the decision-making processes and brought in only to implement the decisions of others. Let us consider how proactive the Training Professional in this case study is becoming:

- recommendations have been made about the possible combination of departments
- recommendations have been made about further development of senior managers
- recommendations have been made about changes to the personnel specifications for staff in the drawing office and in buying
- recommendations have been made about how to deal with staff who are ready to move on but where there are no opportunities for this.

Do we detect a note of panic here? Are we possibly suggesting that the Training Professional might be tres-passing into other professionals' territory? Yes we are, because we believe that one of the problems that has dogged the training function is that it seems to be pigeon-holed into a very narrow definition of the training role. More than ever in today's world of rapid and major change there is a need for Training Professionals to:

- take a wider view
- involve themselves as much as possible in all aspects of the business
- be seen as part of the team addressing the performance needs of the human resource assets of the business.

However, that does not mean that there is not a need for

for sensitivity on these issues, the message is — sell to all concerned the advantages to the organisation of the Training Professional taking on this wider role and having this greater involvement.

Conclusion

So, succession planning is another valuable tool to help the Training Professional to respond ahead of the strategic needs of the business rather than be constantly under pressure from all those same interventions being required yesterday. In the next chapter we look at another important source of rather more immediate information on performance and training needs — the critical incidents that occur in organisations.

Critical Incidents

Introduction

In Chapter 2 we made the distinction between what we called the planned business needs, ie arising out of the stated objectives and strategy of the business, and the unplanned business needs, ie those unforeseen events that buffet a business. The previous two chapters on human resource and succession planning were concerned with the planned business needs, this chapter looks at the unplanned variety. Now these unforeseen events can sometimes be of a positive nature, such as suddenly gaining a major new customer or an existing customer unexpectedly requiring new products or services. However, more often than not these unforeseen events are to do with problems, such as the major breakdown of a piece of equipment, the loss of a major customer, a poor audit result on a particular department or process, a serious customer complaint or sudden large increase in customer complaints. Or it may be an unexpected event completely external to the organisation, such as a piece of legislation or a competitor initiative that needs a response. We are defining these types of occurrence as our critical incidents.

By using the word critical in this way we are saying that these incidents are of significant importance to the business and therefore relate most often to the organisational and occupational/group levels for identification of training needs. However it is possible that the performance of one individual can give rise to a critical incident, for example, a serious accident caused by one member of staff's failure to follow safety procedures. Almost without exception critical incidents, by their very nature of being problems or failures in present performance, identify training for present needs.

A related area is the use of critical incident technique in analysing the gap in performance for individuals. Here the critical incidents are those that occur in a particular individual's job and they are used to analyse the training needs for that individual. This technique is discussed in more detail in Chapter 10.

In Chapter 2 we described these critical incidents as business needs which usually come along with the label 'super urgent, do something quickly'. Throwing some training at the problem is often the almost automatic response to the situation. Since the need is characterised as urgent, that training is then developed in a hurry without a clear understanding of the cause(s) of the problem. Inevitably the resulting training will have unclear objectives and be typical of the shotgun approach to training, ie showering out a load of training pellets in the hope that some at least will hit the target and meet the need. At best this can be a costly and wasteful approach and at worst, totally ineffective.

Until the causes of the critical incident are clearly established then it is difficult, if not impossible, to decide on the appropriate action. Has the incident been caused by a human performance problem at all, or might the cause be faulty equipment or inadequate procedures? If it is a human performance problem, is training the appropriate solution? The first step must be to analyse the problem. Let's look at an example of how this is done using the following case studies.

Case study 4   The disturbing discrepancies incident

At the weekly management meeting of the senior staff of a large department store, the Accountant reports that there was a worrying level of cash discrepancies the previous month. He states firmly that this cannot be allowed to continue and requests (demands?) that immediate training be given to the cashiers on the checkout tills to improve their standards of performance. The General Manager steps in and comments that this is a serious problem and the training department must give it a high priority. Does this sort of situation ring any bells? The Training Professional's immediate response is probably to think 'how on earth do I organise training for 50 cashiers at a drop of a hat?'

However, stop a minute to think about what is happening — the Accountant has very neatly dumped his problem onto you. Is training the best answer or even a solution at all?

The Accountant's request for an improvement in standards of cash handling is obviously an important one. A business need is clearly identifiable. But do we really know what the causes of this particular critical incident are? So what analysis should be carried out? The best way to approach this is to think about the questions which need to be answered:

- What is an acceptable level of discrepancies? In any operation of this nature some mistakes are inevitable and it is only when the level exceeds the acceptable level that action is usually required. This is analogous to the concepts of quality control and use of variances in budgets — action being triggered when the level of faults/expenditure falls outside some agreed band. So first it is essential to determine the acceptable level or trigger point. It may be expressed in terms of pence/£000 of takings.
- In terms of this indicator, is the level of discrepancies the same across all the tills and all the cashiers, or is it concentrated in some tills, groups of cashiers or individual operators?
- If it is occurring with a specific group of cashiers, is there some common denominator, such as being trained by the same instructor? This could highlight the need to look at the standards of performance of the instructors and to examine the systems of training evaluation.
- Is it possibly a fault with the tills themselves? If it is, it could throw up an unexpected training need for the till service engineers!
- Are the discrepancies arising in particular activities, eg in payments by cheque?
- Could the discrepancies be occurring somewhere other than at the checkouts? For example, in the cash office where the takings are checked?
- Could the discrepancies be caused by some other reason than lack of skill? For example, could dishonesty be a cause?

As you can see, the questions, simply by being posed, have opened up a wide range of possible causes of the problem. Already it is becoming obvious that training might not be the appropriate solution at all and even if it is, it may not be necessary to train all the cashiers nor train across the whole range of cashier skills. The process:

- identifies the *exact nature* of the problem and investigates the causes
- ensures non-training solutions are considered
- if training is a solution or part of the solution, it ensures that the training is *focused* on the right people and on the right skills.

Let's look at another example.

Case study 5   The awful accidents

The Warehouse Manager has just taken over a newly built warehouse. The warehouse operatives have all been given additional training to handle the new order pickers that are being used in the warehouse. In the first month of operation, the manager reports that there have been a worrying number of minor accidents and one more serious accident which resulted in a staff injury, all involving the new order-picking vehicles. She is convinced that the training given has not been adequate and wants them all retrained immediately. The Training Professional, yet again, experiences that sinking feeling – this sort of training is very expensive and the budget is already overspent so far this year. The Warehouse Manager reminds you that safety is considered a priority issue in the organisation.

However, you have learned your lesson over the cashiers – you trained them all and then found out that it was a problem with the cash counting machine in the cash office!

This time you are going to analyse the problem. Again, a good starting point is to think of all the questions you need to ask.

- *Who* were involved in the accidents?
- *What* actually happened?
- *When* did they occur?
- *Where* did they occur?

This is the basic fact-finding operation. The next stage is to consider what are all the possible causes of the accidents — this is almost a brainstorming exercise, since sometimes the cause may turn out to be very unexpected. Could it be:

- operator performance error (the hot favourite with the Warehouse Manager)?
- a fault with the order-picker equipment?
- a problem with the design of the warehouse?
- a weakness with the supervision of the operators?
- a problem with the way the stock is being stacked?
- vandalism of any sort?

Even if it turns out to be operator performance error, go on questioning:

- Is training the answer, for example:
  - Could a rewrite of the manual or operating procedures be the answer?
  - Are the staff suitable for this type of work?

- If training is the answer:
  - Do all the operators need retraining?
  - Do they need complete retraining or only in certain skill areas, eg reversing the order-picking vehicle?
  - What was wrong with the previous training, was it poorly designed or poorly delivered, and does this have any implications for who does the retraining?

Let's recap on what you have done. Just as with the Case study 4, you have:

- identified the *exact nature* of the problem and investigated the causes
- ensured non-training solutions are considered

- if training is a solution or part of the solution, ensured that the training is *focused* on the right people and on the right skills.

Monitoring whether the solution has worked is usually not hard with critical incidents of this type. The business need is clearly defined − the level of cash discrepancies should return to normal, and the accidents should cease. Sometimes it will be important to continue the monitoring for a long period of time. It is possible that giving attention to the problem has in itself had a short-term effect. If dishonesty was the cause of the cash discrepancies it is quite likely to stop for a while; if the warehouse operatives have been larking about, this too is likely to stop once an investigation is under way.

Again do we hear a note of scepticism − all this analysis is fine in theory, but in the real world there is simply not the time. This chapter started out by saying these were usually business needs that came along labelled 'super urgent', is there not a danger of analysis paralysis and nothing getting done? The answer to this quite justifiable concern is fourfold:

- You need to ensure you get all the help that you can from the people that can provide it, eg the Accountant and the Warehouse Manager. It will be important to sell the idea that it is a team effort. You remember that we referred to the Accountant dumping the problem onto you. Make sure that there is appropriate ownership of the problem and appropriate ownership of the analysis − this should lead to the appropriate ownership of the solution.
- A proper analysis of the problem and identification of causes, will help make the development of any training solution a quicker process as well as a better one.
- The right solution may well turn out to be a quicker option than the original training solution proposed and therefore the overall process may turn out to be shorter.
- Can you afford to delivery the wrong answer?

This last point is a very important one − it is not only your training budget that we are talking about, but your credibility as a Training Professional and the credibility of training overall.

Conclusion

In this chapter we have discussed the identification of training needs from what might be described as one-off (and, by our definition, critical) incidents. In the next chapter we look at the sorts of training needs that can be identified from the regular, routine reporting from management information systems.

6

Management Information Systems

Introduction

There are many weighty tomes that set out to describe the purpose of management information systems (MISs) and how they should be designed and implemented. The purpose of this chapter is not to cover this rather specialist ground but to examine how the Training Professional might use an MIS to assist with the identification of training needs. However, before we begin it is important to establish what we mean by an MIS. Lucey (1991, p 2) says that an MIS can be defined as:

> A system to convert data from internal and external sources into information and to communicate that information, in an appropriate form, to managers at all levels in all functions to enable them to make timely and effective decisions for planning, directing and controlling the activities for which they are responsible.

He quite rightly emphasises the *use* of the information, not how it is produced, and that use being for *decision making*.

In our earlier book (Bee & Bee, 1990, p 3) we too stressed that an MIS should deliver the information that managers needed to do their jobs, by defining an MIS as a system which produced:

> the right information in the right form at the right time, so enabling the manager effectively and efficiently to do his/her job.

However, some writers, for example Hicks (1990, p 78), concentrate on the role of the computer in an MIS. He defines an MIS as:

a formalised computer information system that can integrate data from various sources to provide the information necessary for management decision making.

Each of these definitions has something to offer. It is clearly important to focus on the purpose and use of the system. However, the reality of the situation is that the volume of data processed in all but the smallest organisations requires the use of computers to store and analyse the data, so the design of the computer system becomes a very significant factor. The advent of the computer has been of enormous benefit in that it has given managers access to large quantities of information. However, in this very advantage lies the root of many of the problems with the use of MISs. Quoting again from our earlier book (Bee & Bee, 1990, p 9):

Ackoff as long ago as 1967, in a classic article 'Management Misinformation Systems' argued that most Management Information Systems (MISs) were designed on the assumption that managers lacked the relevant information, whereas he believed that most managers suffered from an over-abundance of irrelevant information! Even casual observation of the desks of managers today suggests that Ackoff's message has not been heard ... we still see evidence of the massive piles of computer printouts that hit managers' desks from time to time.

This situation is easing a little with the developments in computer technology that enable managers to choose exactly what information they require and generate only the reports that they actually need. However, the basic problem remains, – the technology has opened up access to enormous amounts of data and it is often very difficult to distil out the key items that will help the managers to do their jobs efficiently and effectively.

Use of an MIS in the identification of training needs

We talked in Section 1 about the importance of Training Professionals continually scanning their environment – an

MIS offers a ready-made systematic method of doing so. It can offer a ready-made window into the business needs arising out of current performance by the business. As an MIS usually reports on aggregate performance, ie by department, factory, region, and for the organisation as a whole, this approach is geared to identifying training needs at the occupational/group and organisational levels. Also, as an MIS reports about the past and the present it is likely that any training needs identified will be present ones. However, there could be occasions when the system identifies a trend for, say, growth in production and where a threshold of work is approaching that will require additional staff, plant and equipment to meet the business needs. In this situation we would be training for the future.

So how does the Training Professional proceed? First, they must think hard about the information they require from the MIS to meet their purpose of the identification of training needs. They must decide what information they really need. There are no easy answers to this and it will be very dependent on the nature of the business. However, some examples of the sorts of performance measures that might be monitored are:

- levels of production output
- levels of sales
- quality indicators, eg wastage rates, defect rates, customer complaints
- productivity indices, eg output/employee, man-hours/ product unit, utilisation of machines and equipment
- accident rates
- labour turnover
- absence rates.

The second key decision is how should the data be analysed, ie what sorts of things should the Training Professional be looking for? Some examples are:

- trends over time
- variances from targets
- comparisons with norms, eg particular departments with

48

the organisation norm, the organisation with industry norms or national norms.

Let's look at some small case studies to illustrate the usefulness of an MIS as a link between the business needs of the organisation and training needs.

Case study 6   The disappointing department

You have noted that over a period of time that there has been a regular shortfall against production targets in Department X. What might be the reasons for this:

- staff underperforming, because of:
  - poor productivity?
  - poor motivation?
  - poor supervision?
- problems with machinery?
- problems getting raw materials?
- disputes?

Some of these *could* indicate a training need, for example:

- to improve the skills of the production operatives and hence increase productivity
- to improve the supervisory skills
- to improve the skills of staff who maintain the machines
- to improve the skills of the staff dealing with the ordering of raw materials
- to improve management skills in dealing with low motivation or the handling of disputes.

Case study 7   The revolting region

You have noted that Region X has had above average labour turnover rates for the last three months compared with the organisation as a whole. The reasons for this might be:

- the labour market is particularly buoyant in that area (comparisons with regional norms would help here)
- labour is being shed for planned reasons, eg a downturn in orders
- staff are being dismissed at a higher than average rate
- staff are leaving of their own accord at a higher than average rate.

Some of these *could* indicate a training need:

- for recruitment training to cope with replacing the staff that are leaving
- to improve performance skills to reduce the level of dismissals (if these are related to skill/knowledge deficiencies)
- to improve management and supervisory skills in dealing with poor performance issues, low morale/motivation issues, if this is diagnosed as the reason for the exodus.

Concerns with this approach could be:

- about the extent of the workload involved in and resulting from this process for the Training Professional
- about whether the Training Professional is again going beyond the remit of their role.

The concern about workload is a justified one. However, it is important to remember that the process is all about identifying *exceptional* trends, variances from targets and norms. The emphasis must be on the Training Professional being discriminating, using their judgement on what are the potentially important business needs being identified in this way and prioritising their work and involvement accordingly.

The question of whether the Training Professional is going beyond their remit, perhaps, depends on their definition or perspective of their role and in particular whether they see their role as proactive or reactive. This sort of environmental scan will enable the Training Professionals to *demonstrate* a knowledge and understanding of the business's performance. It will enhance their credibility to perform as full members of the management team rather than as narrow training specialists.

Conclusion

In this chapter we have discussed how MISs can provide a potent addition to our toolkit for environmental scanning. As we see it, information is the key to all business decisions and Training Professionals who choose to ignore the MIS as a provider of the information on which to base their assessment of training needs, do so at their peril. We go on now to look at the information on performance needs which might be gleaned from an appraisal system.

7

Performance Appraisal Systems

Introduction

Performance appraisal systems are generally understood to refer to the regular meetings between an employee and his/her manager to review and assess the employee's performance in the job, identify any action that is needed to improve performance and in some cases as a mechanism to identify potential and future development needs. The process typically consists of:

- a review of performance against specific objectives set for the job over the review period
- a review of performance against general competencies, such as:
  – job management skills, eg planning and foresight, decision making/problem solving ability, resource management;
  – people management skills, eg delegation, control, training/development/appraisal of others, resolution of people problems;
  – personal skills, eg communication/interaction with others, flexibility, motivation of self and others, energy, resilience
- a discussion on any action required to improve performance
- setting objectives for the next review period
- (sometimes) a discussion about potential and future development.

Randell *et al* (1984, p 9), state that:

Some kind of staff appraisal activity goes on in all organisations. It ranges from intermittent, informal and often ill informed discussion between managers about individual members of staff to highly formal appraisal procedures, based on extensive sets of forms and established times, rules and frequency of assessments.

They say that the purposes of staff appraisal procedures vary from *organisation centred* to *individual centred* and are mainly concerned with establishing controls on the behaviour of people or bringing about change in their behaviour by, among other things:

discovering training needs — *by exposing inadequacies and deficiencies* [our emphasis] that could be remedied by training.

The intervening years have taken many organisations a long way from using their appraisal systems for 'exposing inadequacies and deficiencies' to being rather more forward looking and concentrating on performance development in the future rather than dissecting the blame laden past.

Relationship between performance appraisal and TNA

Clearly, the ability of a performance appraisal system to deliver useful information on training needs will depend on the quality of that system. There has been a considerable amount of literature written about the problems with performance appraisals which largely focus on the inability of the manager to make consistent and accurate assessments. Despite these drawbacks and the pocketed nature of the existence of appraisal systems (this is particularly so for blue collar workers) it would appear both from anecdotal evidence and a survey of the training needs literature that appraisal systems are seen as a principal way of identifying training needs in organisations. Indeed Sloman (1993), in an article in *Personnel Management*, commented on the results of a small survey he had carried out on how some of the companies with the best track record in training approached the key training issues:

What came through powerfully, however, was the growing importance of performance appraisal in identifying (training) needs.

Looking at appraisal systems in terms of levels of training needs, their primary purpose is usually for identifying individual training needs, although the accumulation of individual needs can lead to the identification of occupational/ group needs. They will rarely be the best source for the identification of organisational needs. Since the main focus of performance appraisal systems is on current performance, the training needs identified are usually present ones. In as much as the performance appraisal system looks at future development, then the training needs may be future ones.

A very interesting article by Herbert and Doverspike (1990) reviewed the American literature on the relationship between performance appraisal and training needs analysis from 1961 to 1985. They concluded (p 253), among other things, that:

> While the *needs analysis survey literature* [our emphasis] ...
> seems to indicate that performance appraisal data is important for the needs analysis process, the *performance appraisal survey literature* [our emphasis] ... seems to indicate that only small percentages of companies and state governments list needs analysis as an important function of their appraisal systems, and that this function ranks very low among the purposes for conducting such appraisal. This may indicate that few companies and state governments truly perform any type of needs analysis, but that when it is performed, performance appraisal data is viewed as a useful source of information.

They went on to say that they found no reports of proper research studies addressing the use of performance appraisal as a TNA technique. They also found (p 264) that while there was plenty of advice about how performance appraisals should be conducted:

> relatively little literature exists concerning how performance appraisal information should be used for needs analysis, and whether it is empirically successful. In addition, there appears to be a large number of inconsistencies and unanswered

questions in the literature concerned with performance appraisal as a needs analysis technique.

So, where does all this leave the Training Professional — perhaps with the message not to take for granted the usefulness of performance appraisal systems nor rely too heavily on them as a method of identifying training needs? In the other chapters in this section we have concentrated on selling what we see as underrated methods of identifying training needs. We find ourselves in this chapter doing the opposite, of advising caution and emphasising the limitations of the method as practised in many organisations.

Using performance appraisal for the identification of training needs

To make the best use of the performance appraisal system, the Training Professional needs to think about the following issues:

- What is the *quality* of the appraisal system in its ability to generate accurate, relevant and useful information on the assessment of performance?
- What is the extent to which the *design* of any forms, procedures, etc encourage the effective identification of training needs. In many systems, there is a section labelled 'Training Requirements' but are managers encouraged:
  - to clearly show the link between lack of specific performance and a need for action?
  - to consider non-training solutions?
  - to specify very precisely the training need rather than proposing a training course?
  - to indicate the degree of priority and urgency of the training needs identified?
- What is the most effective *intervention* of the Training Professional in the process? Is it to:
  - simply record and action the line managers' requests?
  - to discuss the requirements only when there is a problem of some sort, eg insufficient budget, unclear requirements?

   – to discuss all appraisal findings with line managers to establish jointly the performance needs and the best way of meeting them?
   The answers will depend on a number of factors including, the perceived role of the line managers, the Training Professional's workload, the relationship between the Training Professional and the line managers and perhaps most crucial of all the ability of the line managers to undertake what is in effect a mini TNA on their staff. Many organisations now see training and development as an important part of the line manager role. If this is the case and the main burden for the identification of individual training needs is seen as the line manager's responsibility, then an important issue to consider is the necessary training of line managers in TNA.
● What *systems* does the Training Professional need to set up to action the training needs output from performance appraisal? Potentially, this method generates a lot of information and it is vital that systems are in place to record, analyse, action and monitor the information. There is nothing worse (and how familiar this sounds) than a complaint made by both line managers and staff that nothing has been done as a result of their performance appraisal report.

   Where there are weaknesses in the overall quality of the performance appraisal system and/or the usefulness of the design for the identification of training needs, it is yet another opportunity for the Training Professional to take a proactive role. This is not to underestimate the difficulties of initiating a review or redesign of an existing system. This can be a large and complex task often involving negotiations with a wide range of people, including staff, managers and trade unions. Clearly, the extent to which the Training Professional presses for action must depend on the degree of inadequacy of the system. However, it is in no one's interests, nor to the meeting of overall business needs, to have a system which is inadequately assessing performance and/or identifying training needs.
   The degree of intervention by Training Professionals into

have a system which is inadequately assessing performance and/or identifying training needs.

The degree of intervention by Training Professionals into the performance appraisal process is within their control. However, there may be sensitivity concerns if others feel that in any way their role is being usurped. In particular, the importance of developing good working relationships with line managers cannot be over-emphasised. We are currently working with a company to recruit a new Training Manager, where the prime requirement for the job is the ability to develop productive working relationships with line managers. However, in our experience line managers usually welcome help in an area of their job where they often feel they have inadequate expertise and too little time to address the issues effectively.

Last but not least, ignore at your peril the need to develop systems to deal with the information! However good the process of TNA is, it will be scuppered if there are not effective systems in place to store, action and monitor the results from it. Although manual systems may suffice in small organisations, almost certainly for any larger organisations a computer system will be essential. There are many computer packages on the market, ranging from ones that can be used for the performance appraisal process itself to those that can also be used as databases for the recording of training needs information.

Conclusion

Appraisal systems, standing by themselves or as part of a wider performance management system, can be generators of masses of information on the performance improvement needs of staff in the organisation. The quality of the information, however, will depend on the quality of the system itself and the people operating it. The appraisal system, like the other systems and techniques in this section, identifies that there is a performance need based on a business need. In Chapter 8 we go on to examine whether or not that performance need actually translates into a training need.

8

Is There a Training Need?

Introduction

Throughout the earlier chapters in this section we have constantly referred to the importance of not seeing training as the panacea of all ills or in this case all business needs! In fact we have advocated that non-training solutions should positively be sought and examined before proceeding down the training path. It may seem strange in a book that purports to be about training and is aimed at those with a particular interest in training to be apparently urging non-training interventions. We are not in any way seeking to undermine the role of training nor put the Training Professional out of a job! Training solutions often require a substantial investment of resources and do not always provide a quick answer. Also, training may not be the right answer and at worst make no impact on the business need at all.

This view is supported by Smith and Delaheye (1988, p 9) who go as far as saying that the mere inclusion of the word *training* in TNA presupposes the nature of the solution that will be proposed. Because of this it is often better to drop the word training and perform a needs analysis.

Regalbuto (1992, p 30), too, says that a lack of skills or knowledge is only one possible cause of a performance gap and that other possibilities include:

- problems with raw materials, equipment or workspaces
- lack of money or staff
- poorly designed work methods
- insufficient motivation.

We have emphasised the need to:

- analyse the business need very carefully

- consider a wide range of solutions
- assess the potential solutions against the criteria of
  - will it effectively meet the business need?
  - will it meet the business need at the lowest cost?

Mager (1991b) suggests that among the range of solutions considered should be the *do nothing* solution and indeed that the first stage in analysis should be to ask the questions, 'Is it important? What would happen if the need was not met?'

This is not to say that there will not be those occasions where, for internal political reasons or as a loss leader, a choice will be made in favour of a training solution. There will be occasions, for a variety of reasons, where the purist will be subordinated to the pragmatist – and rightly so. It may be that training is being used for another purpose than to meet a performance gap. Perhaps it is being used as a morale booster or the opportunity to give the troops a nice time after a particularly tough period. Indeed one of our clients actually stated this as one of their objectives for a particular training programme. We hear the purists shudder, but this is fine – this becomes the business need or at least part of the business need. Our point is that the choice is then made knowingly and can be defended if necessary.

In the rest of this chapter we set out some alternatives to training, based in part on Boydell (1990), and in no particular order, that might be considered before the Training Professional rushes off to produce a training solution.

Improving methods of work or procedure documentation

The methods of work or rate of flow of materials can seriously handicap the employee's ability to perform to standard. One classic story in this field is reported in Robbins (1988, p 33). Here, F W Taylor, the so-called Father of Scientific Management, is reported as noticing that every worker used the same-size shovel, regardless of the material being moved. Taylor thought that if there was an optimum weight that would maximise the shovelling over the course of the day, the size of the shovel would vary depending on the density of the material being moved. After extensive experimentation he found that 21 pounds was the optimum shovel capacity. To achieve this weight when shovelling iron ore a small shovel would be used; to achieve it when shovelling light material such as coke a large shovel would be used. Needless to say, the result was a significant increase in worker output. Using similar approaches to other jobs, Taylor was able to define the one best way of doing each job. In other words, if the method was wrong, no amount of training would put it right.

Another source of problems can be the inadequate documentation of the systems and procedures in use. This, in itself, is not necessarily a problem so long as staff have time to gain the experience required to become a *qualified worker*, ie one who knows how to do all the tasks in a particular job to a defined standard of, say, accuracy or time, or both and there is someone available to coach them on the job. However, where there is more than a modest level of turnover of staff, there is the danger that the knowledge of how to do the tasks in the most productive way will be lost and the availability of resources to coach become severely stretched. Employees in these situations often struggle along as best they can or resort to frequent interruptions of their supervisor when they are presented with a query. It is easy in these situations for a demand to be made for training courses to be set up for the new staff or poor performing existing staff.

A highly effective alternative to training can be to document the proceses and procedures clearly, as in the requirements for the award of certification for British Standard 5750 or its international equivalent ISO 9000. Once the documentation is in place the ongoing costs are limited to keeping it up to date. Such documentation might contain one or more of the following:

- Procedure narrative – a written presentation in logical

sequence of the steps and operations in the procedure. This narrative might be described in some organisations as a 'procedure record' or 'operating instruction' and although the amount of detail will depend on its purpose it is helpful to have a standard layout for the different procedures in operation.

- Flow chart — a pictorial representation of the flow of work or activities.
- Some form of fault-finding or help manual.
- Quick reference manual — similar to those provided by the computer software companies to help the computer illiterate avoid the need to delve into their weighty tomes.
- Information packs — containing details, for example names, addresses and telephone/fax numbers, of people and/or organisations who are involved in the procedure either as suppliers or customers.

The above is not intended to say that no training is required for the newcomer or poor performer but clearly the process is shortened and simplified if the procedure is clearly laid down. The Training Professional can be ideally placed to commission or contribute to the systematic documentation of procedures.

Communication briefings

Sometimes called team briefings, communication briefings by the immediate supervisor or manager can be a very effective method for briefing and instructing employees on changes in methods of work or changes in standards of performance. They can also be used to introduce new procedure documentation or changes to existing documentation. This approach will often shift the need away from the primary need, for example running training courses on the procedures, to training supervisors in how to plan and run effective communication briefings.

Use of technology

Technology changes are taking place at an ever-increasing rate. Developments in microchip technology are bringing down both the cost and size of equipment available in the workplace. Obvious examples are the proliferation of personal computers and their associated software, the use of sensors to control the environment in which we work and the use of computers to control the machines that produce our goods.

Sometimes a skill that has been particularly prized in the past becomes virtually redundant due to the changes in technology. For example, secretarial skills such as shorthand have been much prized. Improvements in the technology of recording and transcribing machines in the 1960s and 70s rendered training to a high level of shorthand skills less necessary for secretaries. The development of voice and handwriting recognition by computers for subsequent conversion into typed text could render shorthand skills completely obsolete.

We have used the example of shorthand training as an example of how new/improved technology can revolutionise the need for a particular skill in the workplace, but other examples abound: machines are taking over many of the traditional skills in manufacturing, the office has been transformed by the PC and the fax, inventory control in warehouses is governed by sophisticated computers and the actual movement of stock has been taken over by robotic systems, and armchair shopping is with us.

Again, this does not necessarily mean that no training will take place. However, the focus for that training will be very different — it will be training people to use the new technology, to maintain these increasingly sophisticated machines and to manage the technological process. There can be little doubt that training in new and changing technologies is a major growth area and it is important that the Training Professional keeps up to date with these developments.

Redesigning the job

Where performance in a job is not up to standard, it is always an option to change the requirements of the job. This is not unusual and in any dynamic organisation the job responsibilities are changing all the time. It may be something as simple as rearranging the tasks that make up the job or it may be something more complex such as developing teamwork where previously the job had been done on a solo basis. Boydell (1990, p 12) suggests that it might be appropriate to look at the standards to see if they have been set too high. Taylorism (Robbins, 1988) was very much about changing the requirements of the job to improve productivity, often de-skilling them and reducing them to a series of simple repetitive actions. Mager and Pipe (1991, p 25) support the view that changing or simplifying what people are required to do is a realistic alternative to changing (training) the skills of the person.

Changing personnel

The alternative to redesigning the job is to change the people doing it. This could be as dramatic as dismissing the person if it can be shown that they are unwilling or incapable of gaining the competencies needed to perform the job to an appropriate standard. Actions short of dismissal could be transfer or redeployment to other work or transfer temporarily to other, less demanding work while the competencies are developed.

Perhaps the employees have the skills to do the job and the change that is required is to improve their motivation. This could be linked to the immediate work environment, for example the role, skills and attitude of the supervisor or of the peer group. Again this may highlight secondary training needs − training for the supervisor in leadership skills or the whole work group in developing teamwork skills.

Dealing with organisational obstacles

In addition to the job not being right for the person (redesign the job) or the person not being right for the job (change the person), it is always possible that organisational constraints might be responsible for the poor performance. The insertion (or removal) of a layer of supervision, amalgamating sections into a department or the separation of sections from a department are examples of organisation structural change that might be considered. Other possible organisational obstacles could be the communication systems, the financial systems and/or the physical environmental factors such as noise, temperature, lighting, etc.

Conclusion

In any given situation there will be a range of possibilities that might be considered as options capable of being tested against the business needs. We are not suggesting that non-training solutions will always be better than training solutions, but that other options should be considered for their cost effectiveness and timeliness of implementation. If such an approach can be shown to be more effective and/or cheaper, end the analysis there and implement the non-training solution. This means that the Training Professional is then able to target his/her skills directly on those activities where there is the highest return for the investment made and not fritter away their resources on ineffective and costly training events or perhaps non-events!

So, we have looked at a range of sources of information that is around us, a range of windows into the business needs. We have emphasised the importance of analysing the business need very carefully so as to identify the appropriate course of action. We have also emphasised the need to examine non-training interventions to see whether they can provide a more effective solution to the business need than can training.

In the next section we go on to look at how, having

identified a training need, we *specify* it very precisely so that the training can be focused and directed at meeting the business need.

Section 3
Specifying Training Needs

Introduction

In the Introduction to the book we defined training needs analysis as the process encompassing the three stages:

- identifying the range and extent of training needs from the business needs
- specifying the training needs very precisely
- analysing how best the training needs might be met.

Section 2 has taken us around the first section of the Training Wheel — translating business needs into training needs. It described the ways in which the Training Professional can take a proactive and systematic approach to identifying training needs. It emphasised that the process was in two stages:

- identifying the need for the improvement in performance or addition to the competencies of the business's staff
- identifying which of these needs require a training intervention.

Having identified that a training intervention is required, this section is about specifying that training need very precisely. The more precisely the training need can be specified, the more focused can be the training. This in turn will ensure that the training will actually meet the original business need and in the most cost-effective way. We suggest in Chapter 9 that the starting point should be that the job or relevant part(s) of the job should be clearly defined in terms of the competencies required to carry them out. These competencies can be expressed in terms of knowledge, skills or attitudes. We propose a format for what we call a *job specification* which sets out these competencies against their key tasks and includes the standards and measures against which performance can be assessed.

Having specified precisely what is required in the job we

go on in Chapter 10 to look at ways in which we can establish what is the gap in performance between the requirement and the current performance. A clear and detailed assessment of the performance gap will provide the sound foundation for specifying the training both accurately and precisely.

Before we do so, let's take a look in Figure 3.1, to see the place that specifying training needs takes in the Training Wheel.

Figure 3.1
The Training Wheel – Specifying training needs

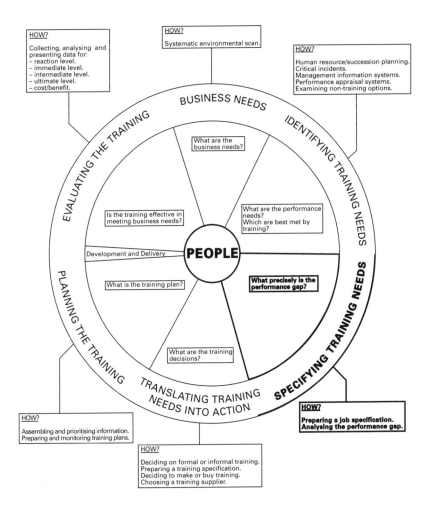

9

Job Specifications

Introduction

Traditionally job analysis has been used to describe the process of obtaining information about a job. Pearn and Kandola (1993, p 1) have redefined the process as job, task and role analysis and described it as:

> any systematic procedure for obtaining detailed information about a job, task or role that will be performed or is currently being performed.

Armstrong (1991, pp 325–6) distinguishes between:

> basic information about the job under the headings of the job title, reporting relationships, overall purpose and principal accountabilities and tasks or duties.

ie the job description and

> the education, qualifications, training, experience, abilities and personal qualities job holders require to perform the job satisfactorily.

ie the job specification.

So a job specification has a very different emphasis from a job description. It is specifically concerned to set out what a job holder has to be able to do or the competencies required to carrying out the job to a prescribed standard. We use the term competencies with some trepidation. Competencies is a word much bandied about at present and often with different meanings. In our view, one good definition (Woodruffe, 1992, p 17) is:

> A competency is a set of behaviour patterns that an incumbent needs to bring to a position in order to perform its tasks and functions with competence.

He lists a set of generic competencies that include breadth of awareness, incisiveness, drive to achieve results, etc and distinguishes between behavioural competencies and what he describes as technical skills, knowledge and abilities required specifically for a job. In preparing a job specification we will use the term competency to embrace both the generic behavioural dimensions and the specific knowledge, skill and attitude dimensions.

Purpose of job specifications

The job specification defines the job, or part of the job, clearly in terms of its purpose and key function, the key tasks and the competencies required to carry them out to specified levels of performance. It is only when the job specification has been carried out that the gap in performance, which might be the whole set of competencies if it is a new job or job holder or a specific set of competencies, can be identified and provide the basis for the formal specification of training. In our view, job specification is a crucial step in TNA and we neglect this phase at our peril.

While recognising that job specification can have a role to play in activities other than in training (eg recruitment, job evaluation) it is the detail into which it goes that is important for TNA. It serves its purpose through cascading down the detail from an overall description of what the job is concerned with, through to the measures and standards against which the job holder is assessed − leading to the identification of performance gaps and hence a precisely defined training need.

How to prepare a job specification

The most common way of preparing job specifications is to interview current job holders and their managers. However, they can be prepared using a variety of other methods. One way is to observe qualified and experienced job operators carrying out their work. Another is actually to do the job.

Some years ago the Local Government Training Board, when designing a new training programme for rat catchers had one of their staff go through the existing training and then practise the art of rat catching under supervision, prior to writing the job specification! Not surprisingly, many of the methods that are used to prepare job specifications can also be used for analysing the performance gap. These methods are covered in detail in Chapter 10.

Stages and structure in writing a job specification

The stages and structure in writing a job specification may vary from organisation to organisation but they generally follow a format similar to the one set out below. These are:

- writing a role definition
- specifying key tasks
- specifying key competencies for each key task
- specifying performance standards and measures for each key competency.

Writing a role definition

A role definition answers the question, 'Why does this job exist?' It states the purpose and main function of the job. Here are some examples of role definitions:

- To ensure the provision of the highest standards of customer service, revenue control, and safety in stations (purpose) by managing operational staff; responding to public inquiries; interfacing with revenue control staff; managing contractor compliance with cleaning, maintenance, and safety standards; maintaining station equipment; and managing incidents (main function).
- To keep plant and equipment, electrical and mechanical systems in working order (purpose) by performing preventive, casual and overhaul maintenance to specified safety and quality standards (main function).

- To provide a high standard of secretarial and administrative support to the directorate (purpose) by planning and organising diaries, preparing agendas and minutes for meetings, filing and retrieving documents and word processing documents (main function).

Specifying key tasks

Specifying the key tasks answers the question, 'What are the important parts of this job?' While the number of key tasks will vary according to the needs of the job, they will usually be the six to eight most important tasks or functions performed in the job. It is our view that if a job has considerably more than eight key tasks then some sort of job review might be indicated.

Table 3.1 sets out some examples of key tasks.

Table 3.1

Key tasks

Key tasks		
Check tickets, passes and permits in order to detect fraud and prevent fare evasion.		
Carry out regular health and safety audits.		
Prepare minutes for all management team meetings.		

Table 3.2

Key tasks and key competencies

Key tasks	Key competencies	
Check tickets, passes and permits in order to detect fraud and prevent fare evasion.	Question customers courteously but assertively. Recognise validity of all tickets, passes and permits for travel, use of car parks and other company facilities.	
Carry out regular health and safety audits.	Demonstrate knowledge of relevant H&S issues, including legislation. Complete H&S checklists on a quarterly basis.	
Prepare minutes for all management team meetings.	Ability to listen effectively and distil out key issues. Write clearly and succinctly. Liaise with members of the management team.	

Specifying key competencies for each key task

The key competencies answer the question, 'What does the job holder need to know or be able to do to perform each of the key tasks?' Some key tasks may have more than one skill, knowledge or attitude competency associated with them. Table 3.2, opposite, sets out some examples of key tasks with their associated key competencies.

Specifying performance standards and measures for each key competency

Standards and measures answer the question, 'What is the acceptable level of performance in a key competency and how do I know when it has been achieved?'

Standards. Two sets of standards may need to be established:

• level of performance at the end of training
• level of performance when a person is fully competent on the job.

Sometimes these will be one and the same, where there is a difference between the two this is attributable to the learning curve on the job after training.

For the purposes of a training specification (see Chapter 12) the standards of performance expected at the end of the training are key outcomes. Clearly, the ultimate levels of performance for full competence must be also established at this stage.

Measures. The measures should be something tangible that can be observed on the job and be capable of measurement. Sometimes they will be an absolute measure (ie 100 per cent), for example 'Documentation completed accurately within one week of the date to which it refers.' On other occasions they will allow for some tolerance, for example '80 per cent of queries will be resolved within 48 hours of receipt.'

Table 3.3
Key tasks, key competencies, standards and measures

Key tasks	Key competencies	Standards and measures
Check tickets, passes and permits in order to detect fraud and prevent fare evasion.	Question customers courteously but assertively.	Achieve an average score of 80 per cent on evaluations by an observer using a checklist of courteous and assertive behaviours.
	Recognise validity of all tickets, passes and permits for travel, use of car parks and other company facilities.	During spot checks by the manager, recognise tickets, passes and permits in face-to-face contact with customers at a 90% accuracy rate.
Carry out regular health and safety audits.	Demonstrate knowledge of relevant H&S issues, including legislation.	Achieve a score of at least 80% on H&S test conducted at regular intervals without warning.
	Complete H&S reports on a quarterly basis.	Documentation completed accurately within one week of the date to which it refers.
Prepare minutes for all management team meetings.	Ability to listen effectively and distil out key issues.	Draft minutes completed, requiring a maximum of 2 substantive amendments and 5 drafting amendments, within 24 hours of meetings.
	Write clearly and succinctly.	
	Liaise with members of the management team.	Final minutes agreed and circulated within 48 hours of meeting.

Table 3.3, opposite, sets out some examples of key tasks, key competencies and associated standards and measures.

Conclusion

So we now have a very detailed description of how the job translates from its role definition through to the measures and standards that are appropriate for the effective discharge of the principal duties. This provides the yardstick against which any performance gap will be established. Some organisations are using the appropriate levels of NVQs/SVQs as a way of specifying or categorising the competencies needed in the job. They can provide the basis for identifying the performance gap between current abilities and the level of competence needed. In the next chapter we look at a range of methods and techniques for identifying and specifying the performance gap.

10

Investigating the Performance Gap

Introduction

So far we have identified that there is a business need requiring some form of intervention and that training is likely to be the best way of addressing the need. We are now at the stage of deciding what sort of training is required, ie specifying our training requirements. The more precise and detailed we can be about the requirement, the easier it will be to develop and deliver training which is focused and directed to meeting the business need in the most cost-effective way. This chapter discusses a range of approaches to how we set about investigating the performance gap. Many books (Kubr & Prokopenkpo, 1989; Stewart & Stewart, 1978) structure these approaches under the levels of training need, ie organisational/group/individual. However, so many of the methods can be applied to more than one level that this division does not always appear helpful to us. We prefer to present them as a portfolio of techniques providing sufficient detail about what they are and how they can be applied to allow the reader to choose the most appropriate technique(s) to meet their needs.

In deciding whether there is a performance gap to be remedied, Olivas (1983, p 19) suggests that at one end of the spectrum in some organisations it is the rule rather than the exception for senior managers simply to state their thoughts as to what training is needed, because it is traditional to offer certain forms of training or because other organisations are doing it. At the opposite end of the spectrum, other writers (Steadman, 1980, pp 56−61; Ferdinand, 1988, pp 29−30) describe various techniques by which the Training Professional might proceed to investigate the performance gap.

The techniques are, of course, all different ways of gathering data on job performance. As such, they can generally be subdivided under the four major approaches to data gathering:

- observation
- interviews
- self-complete questionnaires
- desk research.

We have chosen to group the techniques in this way as a means of helping readers to find their way through them; we are aware that some of them could be located in more than one group. Table 3.4 sets out the list of techniques. Each technique is then described in turn below. As we indicated

Table 3.4

Techniques for assessing job performance

Data gathering approach	Technique
Observation	Direct observation Work samples Simulations

Interviews	General 1 – 1 interviews
	Performance appraisal
	  interviews
	Non-directed counselling
	  interviews
	Critical incident interviews
	Repertory grid interviews
	Other structured interviews
	Group discussions

Self-complete questionnaires/reports	Questionnaires Diaries/logs Tests Psychometric tests Self-reports/assessments
Desk research	Document/records analysis
Combination(s)	Key person consultation Assessment/development centres

in Chapter 9, many of the techniques can be used to gather data for job specifications as well as providing information on the performance gap.

Observation

Direct observation

Observation of people in the workplace is perhaps the most obvious approach to gathering data on job performance. As a technique it can range from the use of detailed techniques such as the work measurement and method studies of the management services/work study officer to relatively unstructured studies of simply observing a colleague in the workplace. In the work study observation, precise recordings are made of all activities, including the times of these activities, and the tasks are *rated*, ie the performance is assessed against a mythical qualified worker performing at the rate of a British Standard worker. At its most rigorous, when and for how long the observation takes place is planned in great detail using time/activity sampling techniques.

A distinction is sometimes made between observation that is directed towards the content of the job, eg noting the time spent answering telephones, number and detail of activities involved in cleaning an escalator, and observation which is looking at behaviours, eg incidence of questioning behaviours, assertive behaviours. This latter approach often involves using checklists of key behaviours to record both the frequency of the behaviours and sometimes a rating of the effectiveness of the behaviour.

Observation has the advantage that it is getting first-hand evidence on the job and how it is performed. It can deliver highly relevant information on training needs at the point where the impact of well specified training will be best felt. It can range from observation where the observers are completely divorced from proceedings, through observation where observer can intervene and question the job holder as appropriate, to the extreme of the observer actually doing parts or all of the job. Depending on the extent to which the subject of the observation is allowed feedback on the results and the opportunity to comment on them, this method provides for the comparison of the inferences of the observer with the views of the observed.

The principal disadvantages of observation as a technique is that it can be very time consuming and hence costly, and that it requires the use of staff who are both highly skilled in the process or system of observation being used and often knowledgeable about the content of the job. Clearly the training of such observers is a complex and time-consuming job in itself. Another disadvantage is the limitation of being able to collect only the information on activities which are visible (as opposed to intellectual). Finally, there is always the problem of the impact of the observer on job performance. The work study officer/rate fixer will at worst be seen as a spy in the workplace. Other observers could well corrupt the activities they are observing by their very presence in the workplace. This is often referred to as the Hawthorne effect after the studies carried out by Elton Mayo at the Hawthorne works of the Western Electric Company in Chicago between 1927 and 1932. Tyson & Jackson (1992, p 44) describe the Hawthorne effect as occurring when the subjects under study change their behaviour because they are being studied.

Work samples

The study of work samples is similar to observation of the people involved except that you are looking at the finished product rather than the way it is produced. The samples can be produced during the normal course of work. Alternatively they can be produced specifically for the purpose of assessing performance – the old-time apprentice's masterpiece on graduation is a good example of this. Other examples might be to examine samples of wordprocessed documents, project reports or training needs analysis studies. In essence you would be comparing these samples against the ideal in order to identify specific errors or areas of weakness. The equivalent for jobs where the *how* is as important as the *what* is done would be, for example, to introduce a customer satisfaction form for monitoring the performance of receptionists/telephonists. The NVQ/SVQ process uses work samples as one way of assembling evidence for assessment.

The main advantage of using work samples as a means of assessing performance is that the analysis usually relies on work that is produced during the normal operation of the job. The main disadvantage is that it can need special content analysis which can only be done by an assessor with special expertise.

Simulations

A variation on observing the job activity or behaviours in the workplace is to set up assessments in simulated conditions. For example, flight simulators are used to test pilot skills in mock emergencies which are set up to assess the ability of staff to handle these situations; role plays can be used to assess appraisal interview techniques. The main advantage of this approach is that they can be set up to simulate situations which do not occur frequently in the workplace such as emergency situations and where observation in the workplace may not be appropriate, such as in a real appraisal interview. However, their disadvantage is cost. Simulation equipment can often be very expensive and simulation exercises are very time consuming to research and develop. There is also the costs of the individual being away from the workplace.

Interviews

The interview, in one form or another, is probably the most frequently used technique for getting at the data in order to specify the required training. Perhaps it is used too much and sometimes without other techniques having been considered, because as a technique it appears familiar and relatively easy to do. In fact using interviews to gather data on job performance requires considerable skill. However, the interview is a very flexible technique in that it can be formal or informal, unstructured through to highly structured, be one to one or involve groups. It can be conducted in the workplace, in private, on or off the job, face to face or by telephone.

Interviews have the advantage that, in the hands of a skilled interviewer, they can reveal vast amounts of data about deficiencies in skills, knowledge, attitudes, feelings, causes of problems and their solutions. They can provide the interviewees with the maximum opportunity to represent themselves spontaneously and in their own terms, especially when conducted using open and non-directive questioning techniques.

The main disadvantages are that they can be time consuming to carry out and to analyse. The very strength of the open question and unstructured interview in obtaining a rich supply of data from the interviewees is in itself a weakness when the analysis takes place. The need to summarise the information, grouping the data into categories, means that much of the original richness can be lost. With more structured approaches you lose some of the initial richness but this can be compensated for by easier and sometimes more productive analysis.

Also, interviewing is a skilled business requiring many hours of training and practice to be able to establish rapport with and gain the interviewees' confidence so that together the interviewer and interviewee can generate data without generating feelings of resentment, suspicion or embarrassment. Another difficulty is one rather akin to the Hawthorne effect with observation techniques − the problem of what is called interviewer bias. The way an interviewer actually asks the questions may have a significant impact on the answers. This can range from the overt leading questions to more subtle and sometimes unconscious effects of body language. This can be a particular problem when the issues being discussed are sensitive ones and where there might be perceived right or expected answers. Bias can also creep in to the recording of the answers as well. Training and the use of more structured approaches can help reduce this problem.

Interviews can range from:

- the *unstructured* type where the aim is to allow the

interviewees as much freedom and as little constraint as possible in providing the data. These types of interview are most helpful when trying to look at attitudes, flush out problems, etc.

- what might be called *semi-structured* interviews, where the interviewer has a predetermined structure in terms of areas to cover and sometimes specific questions to ask. These can be designed for the specific purpose of the study or be standard in format, for example using an appraisal questionnaire.

- through to *highly structured* approaches such as using repertory grid and critical incident techniques.

A range of these types of interview is discussed below.

Performance appraisal interviews

Performance appraisals are perhaps the commonest form of interview used to generate data on the performance gap. One of their major functions is to assess past/current performance and identify where action may need to be taken to improve performance. The use of appraisals for this purpose at least implies that the process is systematic but on the whole it is only as good or as bad as the appraisal process itself. Often appraisal schemes are introduced for a particular purpose and this purpose may not be compatible with the interviewee *confessing* to or accepting there are any faults that require the remedial act of training. This can be particularly so where the primary purpose of the appraisal scheme is to help in the allocation of pay rises.

One advantage of the appraisal scheme in specifying the training that is required is that it has a degree of face validity if the training need arises out of an adult discussion between the appraised person and the supervisor or manager. It also has the advantage that the paperwork is usually designed in such a way that the identified needs are presented in a fairly standard way for aggregation by the Training Professional.

Most of the problems associated with the use of appraisal schemes for the identification of training needs (see Chapter 7) affect their use for the specification of training equally as much. They tend to vary between being very subjective in their assessment of performance and being very mechanistic – measuring only the tangible. The successful assessment and specification of the performance gap depends in part on the quality of the appraisal documentation and critically on the skills of the assessor, ie the manager. Also the next step of specifying the action to be taken to meet the performance gap can be another weak link in the chain. As we discussed earlier in Chapter 7 managers, often through a lack of understanding, skill or time, fail to specify either accurately or precisely the action, which may or may not be training, that is required. It is very tempting for them to opt for a standard training course, rather than specify the particular performance need that is to be addressed. One example of this that we came across was where the director of a local authority housing department decided as a result of appraisal sessions that self-defence courses were needed to help his staff who were subject to physical assaults by the tenants. On opening up the discussion on the business need, he subsequently accepted that training in interpersonal skills and communication skills was really the answer.

Another disadvantage of many appraisal interviews as a technique for specifying training need is that so many appraisal schemes quickly fall into disrepute and staff and managers have little belief in the output from them – simply going through the motions once a year in order to keep the personnel department off their backs. Also, there is a feeling that, once the need for training is written on the appraisal form, in some way it is no longer the responsibility of the manager to see the training through to improved performance in the job, but that of the Training Professional.

Non-directed counselling interviews

Non-directed counselling is similar to performance appraisal in some ways (eg it is carried out in private on a one-to-one basis and requires similar preparation by both parties but, as the name suggests, does not allow for any guidance from the counsellor in terms of what training should be prescribed. It can be very good for generating deep personal data on the training required and is particularly valuable in areas of problems in interpersonal relations. However, it is very time consuming and therefore an expensive way of generating the data and requires well-trained counsellors.

Critical incident interviews

An example of a highly structured interview is provided by the use of critical incident technique. As the name suggests the interview is focused on critical incidents, which are incidents where it is felt that someone had performed particularly well or particularly badly. Having identified such an incident, the interviewee is asked to describe it − the background to the incident, where and when it occurred and what the person actually did that was particularly effective or ineffective. The interviews are usually carried out with a sample of job holders and their managers.

The advantage of the technique is that it is quite easy to undertake and only requires a minimum of training for the interviewers. The disadvantages are that it relies on the individual's memory of events and that sometimes people will tend to remember more of one type of incident than another, eg the difficult ones. Also, sometimes people may be unwilling to admit to examples of poor performance or indeed may not have identified these as such and hence the need for another perspective from the manager.

Repertory grid interviews

One form of a highly structured interview which is (re)gaining some popularity with practitioners is the repertory grid interview. It is based on the Personal Construct Theory developed by George Kelley in the 1950s (Stewart, Stewart & Fonda, 1981). In essence, Kelley identifies personal constructs as a mechanism for getting insights into people's view of the world. In our particular case, it is managers' and job holders' views on what constitutes good and poor performance.

There are many variations on how to conduct a repertory grid interview. However, they are all based around the same theme. For example, a manager is asked to select, say, nine people from the target group and place their names or coded numbers on cards. These might consist of three the manager regards as effective performers, three who are regarded as ineffective and three whose performance is variable. The nine cards are laid out as a 3 x 3 grid. Triads of cards are then picked from which the manager is asked to choose the two that are the most similar. The manager is then asked to describe the aspects of performance that distinguish the pair from the singleton. Skilful questioning is then used to probe the differences to obtain as detailed and as specific a description of the behaviours involved as possible. These differences of commission or omission are noted and the questioning turns to another three and so on. This process is continued until no new differences are being identified. Each comparison identifies the behaviours used or missing which have a significant impact on job performance which can then be used to specify the training for the target group.

Repertory grid techniques can provide a vast amount of detailed data which can be analysed in a variety of ways. The technique is particularly useful in identifying the training needed by people whose jobs are complex and/or are difficult to define (eg managers). Also a major advantage of the technique is that it is claimed that the data obtained in this way is free of the *normal* interviewer bias. However, it does require great skill on the part of the interviewer in guiding the interviewee to the hidden data and skill in analysing the mass of data to produce information that can be worked up to a training specification. An excellent detailed description of the technique itself and its application can be found in Stewart, Stewart & Fonda (1981).

Other structured interviews

Other approaches that are available are, in effect, highly structured interviews. These include detailed and complex questionnaires, eg the Work Profiling System developed by Saville and Holdsworth, and position analysis questionnaire techniques. Many organisations develop their own systems and questionnaires. Pearn and Kandola (1993) give a good introduction to these approaches and other job analysis techniques.

Group discussions

Group discussions resemble one-to-one interviews in some ways in that they can be anywhere on the spectrum of very structured to totally unstructured, formal to informal. The discussion can focus on the job or role analysis for individuals, on group issues or any number of tasks or themes. The group discussion can use any of the familiar group facilitating techniques such as brainstorming, force-field analysis, and consensus rankings.

The main advantages of group discussion are that it permits on-the-spot synthesis of different viewpoints while at the same time building support and ownership for the particular response that is decided upon. It decreases the client's dependence on the service provided by the expert because of their obvious involvement in the process. Another claim for this process is that it helps participants become better analysts of their own training needs which, if true, must be a step forward.

As with all these techniques there are down sides to its operation. By its very nature it is time consuming, and therefore expensive, for both client and consultant. Also there can be difficulties quantifying and synthesising the data particularly where the less structured techniques are used.

Self-complete questionnaires/reports

An alternative to observation and interviews as means of gathering data is the self-complete questionnaire/report. The basic and obvious difference between this approach and the other two is that it only involves the target group and there is no external intervention in the form of an observer or interviewer. The main advantages of this approach are that it is relatively inexpensive and usually quick to carry out, so therefore provides the means to survey a large number of respondents in a short time. Also, if completed anonymously, they give the opportunity for the expression of facts and/or opinions without fear or embarrassment. Since there are no observers or interviewers involved, it removes the dangers of their effects on the process.

Their principle disadvantage is that where questionnaires need to be designed, they often require substantial time and expertise to develop into effective instruments. In addition, they need piloting on a representative sample of the population to be studied, they make little provision for the free expression of responses that the author has not anticipated and they are not very good at getting at the underlying causes of problems that arise or at possible solutions. Traditionally questionnaires which rely on the target population completing and returning them often suffer from limited or low response rates and it may require a considerable effort to ensure both a reasonable level of response and a representative response.

We shall look at a range of techniques which have self-completion as their common theme.

Diaries/logs

These can be set up for the individual to record their activities in various ways. For example, they can be used to record a typical day by listing at regular intervals all the activities undertaken during that period. They can also be used to generate information on critical incidents of the sort described under the critical incident interviews. This approach is particularly useful for jobs where the activities are not easily observable, such as cognitive activities or where the cycle of activities is sufficiently long for observation not to be a feasible approach.

Tests

Tests can be self-administered by individuals or be formally administered to large numbers of the target population and can be used to obtain data on facts and/or attitudes. They can be practical or cognitive.

Tests can be particularly useful in determining whether the business need is caused by a specific missing knowledge or skill competency. Particularly where objective tests are used (ie those with a unique, non-essay type of answer) the results can be easily quantified, summarised and compared with other results. They are usually easily communicated and administered, can be highly predictive of the training that is required and can have a high face validity for those involved because of the practical nature of the test.

They do have certain disadvantages, however. Not the least is the availability of tests which are validated to the specific situation and which measure all aspects of the competencies under review. Also they do not indicate whether the measured competencies are actually being used back on the job. There is also the problem that the results are only as good as the questions that have been asked and there is usually little opportunity for the individual to interact other than by answering the specific question. A further problem is that individuals do not always react well to being tested and this can distort the results. Where the tests are made up of open questions and invite essay-type answers they can be time consuming to mark and analyse.

Psychometric tests

We have chosen to list psychometric tests separately from other tests and checklists. Because of the rigour of their design and the standardisation of their administration they are more objective and produce better feedback than many other tests. In the hands of trained and qualified users they are easy to administer. They can be used to profile individual and group needs. However, they can be expensive in terms of the purchase of test materials and the training and licensing of test administrators.

Self-reports/assessments

Often, in the rush to be sophisticated and trendy in identifying and specifying the training that is required we overlook one of the best sources of data — the individual concerned. Self-reports on training needs can be generated in free form, against a checklist provided or by using some form of self-appraisal questionnaire.

Self-reporting has the advantage of commitment by the persons who are assessing themselves. Through this method it is also easy to obtain data from a wide range of sources fairly quickly and without too much expense. It relies upon the individuals having sufficient knowledge about their present and future jobs to give intelligent suggestions for training. Also an individual's priorities for training may be very different from their manager's/organisation's priorities. Wouldn't many people like to have the opportunity of completing a company-sponsored Masters of Business Administration (MBA) when what their boss wants is for them to be trained, say, to operate the boring old filing system!

With self-assessment the appraisee completes a self-appraisal against the key competencies required in the job. This method can often lead to more precise outcomes required from the training and can be relatively simple to organise. However, Tharenou (1991, pp 46–59) states that while this method may be useful for the specification of technical and specialist training required, her research showed that staff may not perceive the management or strategic training required as well as their managers perceive it. Perhaps this is a case of unconscious incompetence on their part rather than an unwillingness to specify the need.

Documents/records analysis

This form of data gathering is basically using information that already exists and has been collected for other purposes. It is often referred to as secondary research. It can sometimes provide a rich source of data to help specify the training required. For example, an employee satisfaction survey, the primary purpose of which is to provide information on the morale and motivation of the workforce, can also provide invaluable insights into the quality of the management of the workforce. It can effectively provide a form of upward appraisal and perhaps highlight skill weaknesses in communication. Another example could be that a training need has been identified to improve the skills of managers in dealing with disciplinary issues. An examination of the records of disciplinary interviews and industrial tribunal reports could furnish very useful information on the nature of the performance gap and hence the training required.

The main advantage of this source of data is that as it already exists it can be a relatively inexpensive method of gathering information. The main disadvantage is that the data rarely comes in a standard form that can be used directly in specifying training needs. If often needs its own very careful analysis and synthesis into a usable form and the key person consultation (see below) can be very helpful in this process.

Combination approaches

These are approaches that utilise a combination of the above methods.

Key person consultation

Key person consultation is the process of gathering information from persons who, by way of their position and/or status are in a good position to know what are the training needs of a particular group. Key persons can be senior managers, internal/external customers and/or suppliers, other service providers and individuals within the target population. Because of the way in which the key persons are selected for consultation it is sometimes known as contact group analysis. Once the key persons are identified the data can be gathered by use of interviews, group discussions, questionnaires, etc.

This technique has the advantage that it is relatively simple and easy to conduct. It permits an input (and ownership) and the interaction of a wide range of influential individuals each with their own perspective of the needs of the target group. Key person consultation also has the advantage of establishing and/or strengthening the lines of communication between the potential trainees and other stakeholders in the organisation.

In part these advantages carry their own mirroring disadvantages. The use of people such as we have identified above carries with it a built in bias since it relies on the views of people who may see the training needs from their own distinct individual, organisational or professional perspective. Also the 'consultants' need to be carefully statistically selected from across the total range of possible contributors or the resulting picture will be as unrepresentative as the unrepresentativeness of the key consultant group.

Assessment/development centres

Assessment centres for selection have been around for quite some time but their use in identifying and specifying training requirements is a relatively recent phenomenon for many organisations. Woodruffe (1990) goes as far as to suggest that they are a crucial tool for the development of staff. They are, in a sense, the ultimate combination of measures, utilising most of the techniques set out above – psychometric tests, interviews, simulated tasks, written tests, and individual and group exercises. Because of this they can give a very comprehensive analysis of performance measured against requirements and hence identify the performance gap and any required training in a very detailed and precise way.

Their major disadvantage is cost. They need very careful design to ensure that the various tests and simulations accurately reflect the requirements of the job and they require a number of skilled observers who are usually external to the target group. However, during our research we came across one organisation that trained the target work group up to observe their peers with support from an outside consultant — with spectacular results. Finally, the results require careful and often lengthy analysis. Apart from the costs of the observers, there is also the cost of the group being assessed being away from the workplace for periods of not unusually a couple of days. Consequently assessment/development centres are usually restricted to key posts.

They can combine all the best traits of the other techniques and, in the hands of the less competent designers, all the worst traits as well. As in the use of all of the most powerful tools there is the need for the practitioner to know what s/he is doing if more good than harm is to come from the process.

Conclusion

We have listed above many of the techniques or methods of getting at the data to specify the training that will bridge the gap between present performance and required performance. Most of the Training Professionals we consulted in researching this book use only one of the techniques on a regular basis — the appraisal system, with all its known faults, was the one. We are strongly of the view that specification of training needs can be made more scientific and more systematic at the same time by widening the range of techniques used in the TNA process.

Section 4
Translating Training Needs into Training Action

Introduction

You will recall that, in the Introduction to the book, we defined training needs analysis as the whole process of:

- identifying the range and extent of training needs from business needs
- specifying the training needs very precisely
- analysing how best the training needs might be met.

Sections 1 and 2 have covered the first stage of the process – identifying the range and extent of training needs from business needs. Section 3 has covered the second stage of the process – having developed a precise specification of the job and investigated the performance gap. By establishing a very clear picture of what the relevant job requirements are through the job specification and a very clear picture of what the gap in performance is, we now have a very precise picture or description of what the training is intended to achieve. The more precise the specification the easier it is to move onto the final section of the TNA process – looking at what is the best approach to providing that training solution.

At last – you might say – we are about to see some action! Yes, this chapter is about translating those training needs into action. However, do not be tempted to try and skip over the earlier stages, the better the analysis of the need the easier it will be to turn it into action and, what is more, action that will actually meet the business need in a cost-effective way. It will also provide the foundation for assessing the effectiveness of the training in meeting that business need. The more comprehensive and complete the analysis the more secure the foundations for building your training provision.

Enough of this polemic – what next? The first basic decision you will face is whether formal training is what is required or whether some other approach is merited. Chapter 11 looks at formal versus informal training. Chapter 12 is the heart of the process or perhaps, for those of you we have convinced that feelings and intuition have been cast out and prefer continuing with the more concrete building analogy, provides the framework for the (training) building. This chapter covers the preparation of the *training specification*, the vital document that provides the blueprint for how the training is to be carried out and assessed. The training specification then provides the basis for the next key decision in Chapter 13 — the make or buy decision — whether to develop a training course specifically to meet the training need or whether to buy an existing one or perhaps some combination of these options. Finally, Chapter 14 looks at the criteria that might be used for choosing a training supplier.

As in previous sections we see where these activities fit into the whole process by looking again at our Training Wheel in Figure 4.1.

Figure 4.1

The Training Wheel – Translating training needs into action

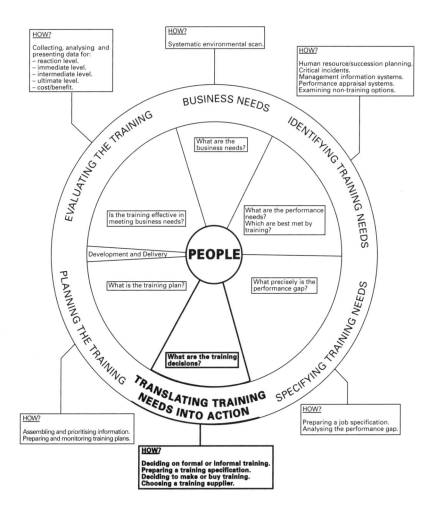

── 11 ──

Formal or Informal Training?

Introduction

It is not the intention of this book to enter into the debate of what constitutes formal training and what does not. We will simply use the definition that when the training involves the intervention of someone outside the immediate work group then it becomes formal training. So, informal training constitutes the sorts of intervention that line managers would make as part of their managerial role of coaching their staff, or a peer member of the work group in helping/coaching others in the group. Now, sometimes informal training forms part of a formal training solution – no problem, but it can never be the other way round as by definition it would become a formal solution.

Formal training

In the last few years there has been something of a revolution in how formal training is delivered. Traditionally, we have usually thought of training in terms of the classroom approach with inputs of information by the Trainer combined with participative elements. You will recall that in Chapter 9 we distinguished between knowledge, skill and attitude competencies. Training may be directed at any one of these, or of course, more commonly a combination of all three. The proportion of the training course involving trainer input is related to the type of competencies that the training is directed. It perhaps can best be envisaged on a continuum as shown below, based liberally on the Tannenbaum and Schmidt (1958) continuum of decision making (see Figure 4.2).

Training courses directed solely at knowledge competencies

Figure 4.2

Trainer input versus participation

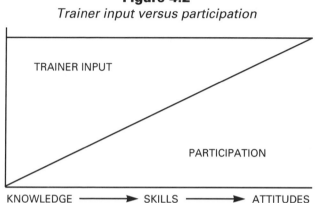

could be, for example, to inform staff about new legislation or new procedures. This sort of training is characterised by heavy trainer inputs. Skills training can range from training for very specific technical skills, eg welding, operating equipment, to the soft skills such as interviewing. This type of training is characterised by a high proportion of time spent on practising the skill, but underpinned by some knowledge input. Training aimed at purely attitudinal changes is probably fairly rare, although training aimed at culture changes is largely of this type. Training addressed at attitudinal competencies is the most difficult and will be characterised by little formal trainer input but which will be heavily delegate focused.

In the 1980s there was considerable movement away from the traditional classroom approach and the Training Professional now has a much wider range of choices available for a formal training intervention. These include:

● Out-of-doors training − this can range from carrying out practically based exercises out of doors (but in a normal environment such as the local streets or countryside) to adventure training in rugged and testing environments of mountains and the sea. These are typically used for the management training in leadership and teambuilding skills.

- Computer-based training (CBT), where the delegates learn by working their way through a predesigned programme. These are primarily used for knowledge competencies, eg learning an administrative procedure or using a computer package. They can also provide the knowledge input of a skill, eg creative thinking. Where the skill can be practised on the computer they also can be used very successfully for skills training, the obvious example being learning keyboard skills. With the development of virtual reality systems (designed to give the user the sensation of being and operating in a real environment), the potential of CBT would seem to be enormous. This is a growing area with the advantage that delegates can learn at their own pace, with self-assessments built in, and in their own time. The limitations are that there is often no inter-delegate interaction and the opportunities and stimulus of learning with others can be lost. An extension of CBT is multimedia training which as the name suggests incorporates other media, eg sound, video, onto the computer-based approach.
- A wide range of distance learning programmes − where the focus is on the delegates working on their own, in their own time, through a package of material which will include inputs of information and exercises. These programmes will usually involve some tutor sessions and sometimes include injections of classroom training for developing the softer skills. They can range from very straightforward, focused training − for example the Police have used it to train staff in the implications of new legislation − to training aimed at long-term development such as a Diploma in Management Studies (DMS) course or a degree.
- Job rotation programmes, where the training is provided by a planned sequence of different job experiences and often supplemented by more traditional training interventions. The classic example of this form of training is the training often given to management trainees. As more and more organisations streamline their management structures by removing layers and the opportunity for development through progression up the ladder is curtailed, forms of job rotation may be used increasingly to

develop staff who have become plateaued, ie reached their peak performance in their current job but with no opportunity for upward progression.

● Job shadowing, often used as part of a range of training interventions, which involves delegates observing or working alongside relevant job holders to gain experience of particular tasks or skills, for example shadowing a manager dealing with a disciplinary issue or preparing a budget.

Informal training

The area of what we have defined as informal training has also developed considerably and a much greater emphasis is being put on line managers coaching their staff. So let's look at when this might be the appropriate solution.

Informal training is appropriate:

● usually for the development of a skill (rather than learning a new skill)
● when there is a need for the training to be tailored to specific work environments
● when the individual responds better to this form of training – some people are frightened of the more formal training approaches
● when there are no suitable formal training solutions available
● when there is a limited training budget
● when the timescale is a problem – either training is required more quickly than a formal solution can deliver or sometimes that the phasing requirements can be more readily met by the more flexible solution of informal training.

Coaching is sometimes seen as a cheap solution. This may appear to be true, in terms that usually it does not come with a readily identifiable cost or cannot be readily allocated to some form of cost or budget centre. However, properly planned and executed coaching can be very demanding of the time of line managers or whoever is doing the coaching.

Also, although we are describing it as informal training, successful coaching requires considerable skills, and itself may give rise to the need for formal training for the coaches. Despite these points, coaching can have a number of positive spin-off benefits:

- it can develop manager/staff relationships
- it develops managers'/coaches' skills
- it can provide great job satisfaction for the coaches
- it can help teamworking
- it promotes a learning environment.

Coaching, although described as an informal training solution, benefits considerably from an element of formality. Clear objectives and a plan for achieving those objectives within a timescale are the ingredients for successful coaching. Coaching can encompass a wide range of different approaches — from the traditional 'sitting next to Nellie/Norman', to project work and the planned involvement of individuals in areas outside their normal work.

The use of mentors as part of both formal and informal training intervention is becoming increasingly popular. These 'trusted advisers' (Oxford Paperback Dictionary, 1979) can play a wide variety of roles from the listening ear, or acting as a sounding board, to taking a proactive role in the development of the individual. Mentors can be line managers but more often are outside the line management function and chosen for their abilities to act as role models and nurture and develop staff. Being a mentor can in itself be a developmental process. Clutterbuck (1991) provides a straightforward and practical guide to the mentoring process.

Conclusion

Consideration of informal training solutions should always form part of the Training Professional's systematic approach to analysing how the training need should be met. If the decision is made that a coaching approach should be adopted, you should not be tempted to withdraw gracefully with a sigh of relief thinking 'another problem solved!' Hopefully it is, but hoping is not good enough — there will need to be some mechanism for establishing that the training need has been met and in turn the business need that gave rise to it successfully addressed. The key to this will be the training objectives covered in the next chapter and the techniques and approaches discussed in the section on evaluation.

──────── 12 ────────

The Training Specification

Introduction

Without doubt preparation of a training specification is an essential requirement for the implementation of all formal training solutions and we would argue, that in a modified form, for all informal approaches. We define the training specification as:

> a *blueprint* or *detailed plan* for the training required to meet the gap in performance and for measuring its effectiveness.

The exact form or structure may vary, but we would suggest that every training specification should include the following information:

- background details of the business need that has given rise to the training need
- description of the target training population, ie the staff to be trained
- the overall aim of the training – a key section which should contain the criteria for assessing that the business need has been met
- the training objectives – another really key section
- the training methods to be used
- the skills required by the trainer(s)
- how the training is to be evaluated (do not be tempted to miss this out)
- the timescale for the delivery of the training
- the venue if relevant
- any other constraints that need to be taken into account.

We will describe each of these areas in turn and there are two sample training specifications provided for you, as Appendices 12.1 and 12.2, at the end of this chapter. Again, the amount of information and degree of detail provided is a matter of judgement − the main guideline is that it should provide:

- a training supplier with sufficient information to prepare a training proposal (see Chapter 14)
- the basis against which the training can be evaluated.

Background to the business need

This part of the training specification should provide a good description of the business need with as much detail as possible of what stimulated the requirement for training. Its purpose is to make sure there is a clear link between the proposed training and an identifiable business need.

For example, the business need could be to respond to a large number of customer complaints which highlighted the poor level of knowledge that the sales staff had of the products they were selling. Alternatively, the business need could be to tackle a high level of wastage of new recruits which on investigation was shown to be as a result of poor interview techniques. More detail may be helpful in these cases − for example, did staff display poor product knowledge across the whole range of products or was it only some products that caused the problems? Had the analysis of the training need shown what particular aspect of the interviewing technique was causing the problem? The business need could be to train staff to meet new legislative requirements, eg on health and safety and on accounting procedures. It could be to prepare staff to sell a new product or handle a new machine.

It may also be helpful to provide some background information on the local context for the training, eg a department or business unit, giving details of:

- the function or principal activity of the unit
- how the unit fits into the organisation structure
- the structure of the unit itself
- size and geographic location(s).

Description of target training population

It, perhaps, seems a statement of the obvious to say that training must be targeted at the people that require it. However, it is surprising how often people are trained in areas that they do not need and, equally, how often some of the people who really do need the training slip through the net. This can mean the training is both wasteful and ineffective − a deadly combination. So, the name of the game here is to identify as precisely as possible the target audience. If the business need has been investigated and analysed fully this information should be readily available.

Next it is important to describe the population. The key information is:

- the projected number of delegates
- jobs/grades and locations
- current levels of knowledge/skill and experience in the area to be trained.

Sometimes it may be useful to provide additional information, eg:

- age profile
- educational level
- previous training
- length of service
- likely attitude towards training.

This last category can be very useful if there are possible morale or motivational problems. Anybody who has carried out training in the midst of major organisational change will be aware how much this can affect the quality of the training experience. If this is known, then sometimes the training can be designed to allow time to address these issues.

Aim of the training

As you will have gathered, this part has a twofold purpose:

- The desired outcome(s) of the training must be stated in terms of the business need, for example, to reduce the customer complaints by X per cent or cut the level of wastage in new recruits to Y per cent within Z months following the completion of training. Sometimes it may prove difficult to provide precise quantitative measures. If this is not possible provide as detailed a description of what the business (or that specific area of the business) will look like after completion of the training. It is surprising how often this very process will reveal measurable indicators. Mager (1991a) provides an excellent and straightforward account of how to turn 'fuzzy' goal statements into well-defined statements of performance.
- Make a clear statement of the change required or standard to be achieved in workplace behaviour, for example, provide a high quality of customer care (as measured against a customer care checklist), manage an emergency situation according to company procedures.

This, in turn, provides:

- the essential introduction to the detailed training objectives
- the essential benchmarks for the evaluation process.

Training objectives

Training objectives are sometimes referred to as *learning objectives* and the two terms can generally be used interchangeably. Training objectives are descriptions of the performance and/or behaviours that you want delegates to exhibit at the end of the training. They are concerned with the results of the training, not the training process itself. They are a vital stage in the TNA process as, if you are not clear where you are going, it is very hard to plan how you are going to get there. The training objectives should follow easily and logically from specification of the business need and aims of the training. It is essential that training objectives are correctly specified because:

111

- the development and delivery of the training will be based on them
- they will form the basis of one of the key stages of training evaluation — measuring whether the learning has taken place
- their clear and full specification will help ensure that the right delegates attend the course
- they enable delegates, their managers and the business prepare for and make best use of the training.

Training objectives must have the following key attributes:

- be focused specifically on the gap between current and required performance
- be expressed in behavioural terms that allows them to be measurable in some way
- be achievable and realistic, but challenging.

They will address the three types of learning — knowledge, skills and attitudes. The usual outcome of training is that delegates gain the ability to do something they could not do before or to do it better. Hence, most training objectives deal with skills competencies and will begin with an action word that reflects a behaviour. Examples of some commonly used action words are:

build, carry out, design, drive, exhibit, make, measure, operate, perform, present, select, set, test, train, use, write.

Some examples of training objectives for skills are:

- to operate a telephone switchboard
- to write a business report
- to build a project network
- to carry out an appraisal interview.

In training, knowledge often supports skill and so some training objectives will deal with knowledge competencies. For example, in a training course on recruitment interviewing

112

the delegates will probably require knowledge of relevant employement law and knowledge of the use of job descriptions and person specifications. They will also need to know the possible ways to structure the interview and arrange the interview room. Sometimes training courses may be solely concerned with knowledge, for example, training for new legislation or new office procedures. Knowledge-based objectives must also begin with action words that reflect measurable behaviours. These are sometimes harder to find.

Some examples of useful words are:

calculate, classify, compare, define, describe, explain, identify, list, name, state.

Avoid words that are difficult to establish measures for, such as appreciate, know or understand. What do we mean by an objective such as 'To appreciate the role of the personnel director'? How do we know or how can we measure whether someone has an *appreciation* of the role of the personnel director? An alternative objective would be 'To state the main functions of the personnel director'.

Some examples of training objectives for knowledge are:

- to list the steps in the procedure for handling a grievance
- to state four benefits of training evaluation
- to identify well-formed (ie that meet the criteria ...) training objectives
- to calculate the duration of a project from a project network using critical path analysis.

Attitudinal change is often a part of a training programme and sometimes an end in itself. It is notoriously difficult to measure and, therefore, requires sophisicated measurement tools. It is often better to target and measure the behaviours that result from particular attitudes. For example if encouraging staff to adopt the equal opportunities policy is the required outcome, then defining objectives such as, 'to conduct a recruitment interview according to the principle of the equal opportunities policy/without gender or race bias' may be the best approach. Mager (1991a) gives a detailed account of how to turn attitudinal objectives into measurable behaviours.

In another excellent book, Mager (1991c) describes the characteristics of a well-formed objective as:

- *performance* – describing what the delegate will be able to *do*
- *conditions* – setting out the conditions (if any) under which the performance will occur
- *criterion* – describing, wherever possible, the criteria or standards for acceptable performance – this may be, for example, in terms of speed, accuracy or quality.

So far, we have concentrated on the performance element. Let's look at some objectives that incorporate all three elements:

- diagnose the fault (performance) in Coldpoint Dishwasher Models 1/2/3 (condition) within 15 minutes (criterion)
- without reference material (condition), state the actions to be taken in the event of a fire (performance) according to the company health and safety policy (criterion)
- make a presentation (performance) to a group of superiors, colleagues or subordinates (condition) lasting 15 minutes (condition) on a work-based topic (condition), achieving an 80 per cent or above score on a checklist (criterion).

How much detail to include in the objectives must be a matter of judgement – it must be sufficient to set out clearly to everyone concerned the intentions of the training in terms of what is expected from the delegates at the end of the training.

Training methods

Training methods usually depend on:

- the training objectives
- the content of the training material
- the target audience.

How much detail is included here is a matter of choice. It may be that as a result of your detailed knowledge and understanding of the three areas above, you will have a very clear idea about how the training should be delivered – at least in terms of the first level of choice. For example as to whether it will involve formal classroom instruction, use CBT, distance learning approaches, etc. On the other hand, it may be that you are not clear as to what might be the most effective approach and want to leave it up to the training supplier to come up with proposals – in which case your training specification should state this.

Sometimes even greater detail is provided, such as specifying the use of case studies or role plays. It may be that a very tight specification is required. However, this loses the opportunity of finding out what the training suppliers actually think are the most appropriate methods. This is one area of the specification where there are benefits to not being too precise at this stage. If the training objectives and the target audience are well specified this should provide sufficient information for the development of the course by experienced and professional training suppliers. Their proposals for the training methods can be a valuable indication of the quality of their 'product' and form one part of the basis for selecting a training supplier – more about this in Chapter 14.

Trainer skills

This is often and surprisingly a neglected area. Sometimes no skills are specified and often only very general requirements are made. Depending on the nature of the course consider specifying:

- precise skills and qualifications – this is often important for technical courses and where a nationally recognised qualification is awarded at the end of the course
- experience of training in the subject area
- experience of training similar types of staff – there is a world of difference between training front-line supervisors and training senior managers!

Methods of evaluating the training

This part is the one that most frequently gets left out. This is for two main reasons:

- many organisations do not evaluate their training either at all, or in any systematic way
- many organisations (dare we say most) do not think about evaluation until the stage when the training is about to be delivered or even until after it has been delivered.

For effective evaluation to take place it is essential that the evaluation methods are designed as part of the development stage of the training. Therefore it is important to include in the specification what evaluation is to be undertaken and who is to carry out any design work. Section 6, Evaluating the Training, sets out details of the approaches to evaluation and the techniques that can be used.

Timescale

It is important to indicate the projected timescale for the delivery of the course and achievement of the objectives. This will be based on:

- the urgency of the business need. Sometimes there will be a requirement to deliver the training as quickly as possible to deal with a current and important performance gap. Sometimes the business need will not require such urgent attention and sometimes the training will actually be to meet a future need and will need to be phased in at the appropriate time.
- practical constraints, such as trainer and facilities availability, delegate availability
- budgetary constraints − when there is money available to carry out the training.

The benefits of providing a timescale are:

- it forces the training specifier to think through the above issues and plan accordingly
- it enables all those involved to be aware of the timescale and to comment if it will not meet their needs
- it allows training suppliers to consider whether they can meet these timescales and prepare a training project plan (a plan of how they will meet the specification in the timescale).

Venue

This is an optional section as specifying a venue may or may not be important at this stage. If it is intended to make use of internal facilities, these may need to be booked. If the course is required to take place in particular locations, eg in regional centres, then specifying this is helpful. Depending on the imminence of the training event, the venue may become a higher priority.

Other constraints

This is an opportunity to include any other limiting factors not already covered, eg:

- maximum number of delegates who can be released at a time
- maximum duration of training
- maximum length of training days
- any cost limitations.

Think carefully about whether and what cost limitations are included. As with the part on training methods, there is a lot to be gained from seeing what the training suppliers come up with. On the other hand, indicating maximum daily rates can sometimes be helpful in targeting appropriate training providers. However, bear in mind the total costs – sometimes suppliers with high daily charges may be able to offer training courses which require very little developmental work and therefore lower overall charges.

Having completed your draft training specification ensure it fully and accurately sets out the requirements for the training by ensuring everyone involved has an opportunity to comment – the training sponsor if one exists, prospective delegates, their managers, subject specialists, etc. This will not only ensure that the specification is right but also gives a sense of ownership to those that have been involved in its development.

Conclusion

Do you always need a training specification? It seems an awful lot of work – I hear the hard-pressed Training Professional cry. There are two particular situations in which this comment tends to arise.

Some people argue that there is no point in preparing a detailed training specification if there is an obvious training course available that will meet the need. However, it is surprising how often the training specification, when compared with the details of the course, highlights significant differences. Now it may be that the existing course will still be used, but it will be used in the knowledge of how far it meets the actual need and allows for consideration of how the areas of unmet need can perhaps be addressed in other ways.

Another argument sometimes used against preparing training specifications is that it is not worth the effort if there are only one or two staff involved or when the training is to be delivered informally. Clearly this is a matter of judgement and depends to a large extent on the type and level of staff concerned. For certain management positions or highly specialised jobs, it will almost certainly be worthwhile preparing a detailed training specification even if only one member of staff is involved. In other situations a shorter, simpler specification may be sufficient. However, we would argue that preparing a specification of some sort is very useful in all circumstances and is a vital step in ensuring that the training solution provides a close fit with the training need.

So far as informal training is concerned, we would argue that, in fact, informal training can benefit as much as formal training from having a training specification. The discipline of having to describe the business need, the aims and objectives of the coaching and the methods of delivery, etc will help ensure that the business need is met.

So what next? We are now ready to consider the choice of whether to make or buy the training, so read on.

Appendix 12.1 Training specification – Customer care course for cashiers

Background

Backland Trading Company Ltd (BTCL) has recently taken over another company, Substandard Ltd. A number of problems have been identified at Substandard Ltd – one of which is that there have been problems between customers and cashiers resulting in both customer complaints and grievances from the staff. In the first three months of the trading year there have been ten customer complaints concerning the poor service offered by the cashiers. Of these only two were concerned with poor technical skills, the remainder concerned their ability to relate positively to customers and handle queries and difficulties. The Branch Manager believes that the poor level of customer service is responsible for sales not reaching expected levels for the time of year. They appear to be running at about 5 per cent below target.

The cashiers are managed by the Duty Checkout Supervisor, who in turn reports to the Branch Manager of each outlet.

As a result of the take-over by BTCL, morale in Substandard Ltd is quite low.

Target population

The cashiers operate checkout tills in five separate retail outlets distributed across the London area. There are 100 cashiers in total – mostly female staff, all on the same hourly rates of pay – 75 per cent are part time on contracts varying between 15 and 30 hours, the remainder are full-time staff allocated to specific shifts. At any one time there are about 10 temporary staff. Most of the cashiers have been with the company for more than two years and have limited experience of other jobs. Most have only basic educational qualifications. The temporary staff are usually students doing vacation work.

All cashiers have received training on the use of the

checkout tills; however, none of them has b
customer care. Their attitude to this training is
as their morale is known to be low, time shou
in the programme to address the possibility of an attitude
issue.

Aims of the training

To provide the cashiers with the necessary knowledge, skills
and attitudes to provide a high quality of customer care so
that:

- customer complaints regarding poor service are eliminated
- customer satisfaction reaches company standards, as
  measured by the company's customer satisfaction survey
- sales are on target.

As poor morale as a result of the take-over is considered a
contributory factor, the training will be expected to address
this issue.

Training objectives

By the end of the course delegates will be able to:

1 explain the benefits of the merger to staff at Substandard
  Ltd
2 explain why customer care is important to BTCL
3 greet and acknowledge customers at the checkout tills in a
  welcoming manner (achieving a minimum score of 80 per
  cent on Part A of the Customer Care Checklist)
4 deal with queries from and difficulties with customers at
  the checkout tills in a professional and friendly manner
  (achieving a minimum score of 80 per cent on Part B of the
  Customer Care Checklist)
5 close the customer transaction at the checkout tills in a
  positive way (achieving a minimum score of 80 per cent on
  Part C of the Customer Care Checklist).

Training methods

The course should be very participative, giving delegates plenty of opportunity to practise skills in realistic role play situations, requiring them to give mutual feedback on their feelings when acting as customers and as staff. Of necessity the training will take place away from the sales floor.

Trainer skills

The trainers will be expected to have had practical experience of dealing with customers in a high pressure retail environment and a track record of carrying out customer care training courses.

Evaluation

A reaction level questionnaire will be used, which will be provided by BTCL. The supplier is expected to undertake immediate level evaluation.

A specialist consultant will be used to design an intermediate level evaluation for implementation by BTCL. Ultimate level evaluation will be monitored against level of customer complaints, customer satisfaction surveys and sales performance.

Timescale

The need is considered to be urgent. It is intended that a decision on the appointment of suppliers will be made by the end of January and it is a requirement that the training is completed by the end of March.

Venue

The training will be undertaken at the well-equipped BTCL Training Centre at Welwyn.

Constraints

A two-day course is envisaged, giving a maximum of 16 hours' training. A maximum of 10 delegates can be released at any one time.

Appendix 12.2 Training specification – Time management course

Background

The Rationalisation Co Ltd (RCL) is involved in the design, manufacture and maintenance of scientific equipment. There is a total workforce of about 400, with about 70 staff with management responsibilities. RCL has recently identified a significant loss of business due to late delivery on commercial contracts. It was estimated that £300,000 (5 per cent of turnover) was lost over a six-month period due to late penalty clauses being invoked by customers. In addition two customers withdrew their business as a result of poor performance on delivery times. An outside organisation was invited in to research the cause of this and, if appropriate, to carry out a training needs analysis (TNA) to specify the training needed to redress the business needs.

The research identified from the staff that the main causes of the problem were:

- interruptions, unplanned meetings, queries and emergencies
- lack of planning/organisation by other people
- shifting priorities
- lack of, or inadequate, delegation
- poor systems for reviewing progress on contracts.

As a result, one of their recommendations is a training programme in time management for all managers in the company.

Target population

There are about 70 staff on management grades, all located at the company offices in Dover. It has been agreed that they will attend within their section/team (Finance, Sales, Production/Distribution) where possible, subject to appropriate cover on the job.

None of the staff has attended formal time management courses although some of them will have covered some of the issues in other management and/or professional training. Some may consider the requirement for them to attend a training course in time management as an insult and therefore they may be resistant to new ideas.

Aims of the training

To provide managers with the knowledge, skills and attitudes required to discharge their duties to appropriate standards in an efficient and timely manner, in order that:

- the cost of late penalty clauses are reduced to a maximum of 1 per cent of turnover in any six-month period
- no customers are lost through poor performance on delivery times.

Training objectives

By the end of the course delegates will be able to:

- identify their current use of time by using time logs, distinguishing between proactive and reactive activities
- select/prioritise daily the right tasks in the right order
- schedule personal planning time on a regular basis
- demonstrate flexibility in their personal plan to respond to changing circumstances
- delegate effectively, achieving a minimum score of 75 per cent on the delegation checklist
- explain the relationship between good time management and good communication
- select and use appropriate time management techniques
- set up effective systems to review progress on contracts.

Training methods

The course should have a ratio of about 1:3 in the philosophical grounding in time management as against practical exercises which demonstrate to the delegates the strengths of good time management practice. It should be a balance of case studies, individual exercises and group exercises and provide some means of assessing current time management practice.

An output should be a delegate action plan which sets out the changes in time management that the delegate intends to introduce over the next six months.

Trainer skills

In order to be credible with the delegates it is essential that the trainers have had substantial experience of management, preferably in a scientific, engineering and/or production environment. They should have a track record in carrying out time management training at middle manager level and above.

The trainers should have good interpersonal skills and be able to involve themselves in fairly robust training sessions.

Evaluation

The supplier will be required to provide a reaction level questionnaire and make proposals for immediate level evaluation. Intermediate evaluation will take place as a part of the formal performance appraisal scheme between the delegates and their managers, when progress against their individual action plans produced on the course will be reviewed.

Ultimate level evaluation will be based on the two indicators included under Aims.

Timescale

It is important that the training effort is concentrated into a fairly short period of time and all 70 managers should have completed the training by July of this year.

Venue

The training will take place in an hotel in or around Dover.

Constraints

Because of domestic commitments of many of the delegates, the course may not be held on a residential basis and must be completed in normal working hours.

13

Make or Buy Decisions

Introduction

We have now reached the stage of having a very clear and comprehensive specification of what training is required to meet the particular business need identified. We next need to consider the options of how the training is to be provided. This is traditionally called the *make* or *buy* option, where:

- the make option involves designing and developing a new course
- the buy option involves using an 'off-the-shelf' course, either:
  - purchased from an 'inside' supplier, or
  - purchased from an 'outside' supplier.

Clearly there may be solutions that lie between these, such as adapting an existing course or developing a new course made up of parts of existing courses.

The choice of whether to go for the make or the buy solution hinges to a large extent on four factors:

- the size of the population to be trained
- the nature of the competencies to be trained
- the timing of the training
- the type of training experience required.

Table 4.1 sets out how some of these factors tend to influence the choice between the make or the buy solution.

The first of these factors involves a trade off between the costs of developing and delivering a new course and the recurring per delegate or per course costs of buying the training. The subject of costs is quite a complex one (see Chapter 16) and the following is intended only as a starting point. Training Professionals wishing to arrive at a comprehensive assessment of the costs may wish to consult their finance colleagues for advice. So, with this caveat, let's look at the costs of buying and the costs of making a new course.

Table 4.1

Choosing the make or buy solution

Factors	Make solution is most appropriate when:	Buy solution is most appropriate when:
Size of training population	Training population is large and the costs of developing a course are less than the recurring per delegate or per course costs of a bought course.	Training population is small and the per delegate or per course costs incurred are less than the costs of developing a new course.
Nature of competencies	Most of the competencies to be trained are company or job specific.	Most of the competencies to be trained are general.
Timing of training	The timing is important as there is more control over timing. Generally needs greater planning and longer lead times.	The training is needed quickly. A greater flexibility of dates is required (assuming a widely available course). Coverage at work is a problem as delegates can only be released in small numbers.

| Type of training experience | There is a need/ advantage in delegates being trained together, eg for teamworking, sharing knowledge or experience. | Delegates will benefit from training with people from other organisations (for an external course) to give a wider perspective, or from other parts of the organisation (for an internal course) or simply the mix does not matter.

Delegates will benefit from being away from their own organisation or colleagues, eg dealing with sensitive issues such as interpersonal skills. |

The costs of buying a course

The cost of the buy solution to meeting training needs is quite straightforward to assess. It is the per person cost of sending delegates away on external open courses, plus any associated travel and subsistence costs.

The costs of developing and delivering a new course

It is easiest to consider the costs for the two elements, development and delivery, separately as the first is a one-off cost and the second is a recurring cost which will depend on the number of delegates that attend the course.

Development costs

Development costs are those costs associated with taking the training specification and turning it into effective training that is ready for delivery and includes the following activities:

- designing the form and structure of the training
- designing the training materials, eg case studies, role plays, games and sometimes videos and computer-based training material where relevant
- preparing pre-course material where necessary
- preparing handouts
- preparing evaluation tools

Now this work is sometimes carried out by external consultants who will charge a consultancy fee and therefore the costs are clear cut. However, sometimes it will be tackled by internal staff, often joint teams of Training Professionals and specialist managers in the area, and in these cases it is important that the development costs are fully logged and recorded. The best way is to institute time sheets and log the time spent by all involved. Usually your finance department will be able to let you have person hour/day costs which will reflect the actual costs, including any relevant overheads, of using those staff. Many organisations choose the internal route and are then horrified, if they actually do the calculation, how expensive it turns out to be. Consultants are often experienced in development work, may have similar courses already within their portfolios and therefore are able to provide a cost-efficient service (more of this in the next chapter).

The next and vital stage in the development process is piloting the course. This is properly a development cost, although if the pilot is successful you have the benefit of having trained a group of delegates! Now the costs for a pilot are very similar to the final delivery costs so let's look at these next.

Delivery costs

Delivery costs are those costs associated with delivering a developed course and are compiled on a per course basis. They include:

- costs of the trainer(s) − these may be fees for consultants, external trainers or guest speakers, or the costs of using internal training staff
- costs of the venue
  - training rooms
  - equipment
  - accommodation, if relevant
  - catering

  (these may be readily identifiable charges from a hotel or training centre or may involve assessing the costs for using internal facilities − seek help again from your finance department)
- costs of duplicated training materials and handouts, and licence fees for use of copyright materials
- administrative costs involved with making the arrangements for the course and the delegates.

In addition are the costs that are common to both bought and made courses − the costs of the delegates themselves, which include:

- costs of delegates' time
- travel and subsistence costs.

The cost of delegates' time would not normally enter into any calculations for comparing the make or buy solutions unless the training was of different durations. This is also the case with the travel and subsistence costs, unless there are differences between the two options. However, these costs should form part of any assessment of the overall cost of a training event, for example as part of an evaluation study.

Sometimes it is possible to get a hybrid solution. An external training provider that runs open courses may be prepared to bring their open course into your organisation and negotiate a fee that is significantly cheaper than the normal charges per delegate. Sometimes the course can be tailored to the organisation's requirements so that you have many of the benefits of a made course but without the heavy development costs.

So let's look at an example.

Case study 8   The fundamental finance training programme

Suppose there is a group of 30 managers for whom a training need has been identified for basic finance training (excuse this woolly language – we do have, of course, a detailed training specification!). The options are to send the delegates on a well-established and reputable two-day course run by Super Training Courses Ltd at a cost of £500 per delegate. The alternative option is to develop your own two-day course. You have had a proposal from a small training consultancy who will develop the course for £3,000. As there are relatively small numbers you are going to regard the first course run as a pilot. You have estimated the costs of delivering the course as follows.

For a course of 10 delegates:		
Trainer costs (using a training consultant)	2 days @ £500/day	£1,000
Venue costs		
● room hire (main training room + 1 syndicate)	2 days @ £100/day	£200

● equipment (a video machine)		£50
● catering (coffees/ teas/lunch)	10 delegates @ £15/ delegate/day	£300
Cost of materials/ handouts	10 delegates @ £10/ delegate/day	£100
Administration costs (based on an estimate of time required and the unit costs of the staff involved)		£150
TOTAL		£1,800

Take the cost of the pilot as the delivery cost of one course, ie £1,800 (if the pilot is successful, this part of the cost is set off against the delivery cost).

See Table 4.2 for a comparison between the two approaches.

Table 4.2
Example of a make or buy decision

	Make solution	Buy solution
Costs	Development costs: £3,000 + £1,800 = £4,800 Delivery costs: 3 courses @ £1,800/course = £5,400 Total = £10,200	30 delegates @ £500/delegate = £15,000
Nature of competencies	Although mostly general competencies, course can be tailored to use organisation's own finance documents/ systems.	General competencies with the advantages of some coverage of different approaches.

134

Timing of training	Training can be delivered three months after need identified due to development time and agreeing suitable course dates with delegates.	Training can be delivered two months after need identified – delegates may appreciate flexibility of dates.
Type of training experience	Delegates able to discuss in depth problems with current budgetary system.	Delegates get a broader appreciation of different systems/ approaches and their problems, by interaction with delegates from other organisations.

Conclusion

The decision will be based on looking at the advantages and disadvantages of each option. Clearly in this case the make option has come out cheaper at £10,200 as against £15,000 for the buy solution. However, what is the training experience that is required – understanding a range of different systems or obtaining a detailed knowledge of the organisation's own system? How important is the issue of timing and flexibility of dates? The training specification should provide the answer to these questions and cost will be only one factor in the decision-making process.

With both the make and buy solutions the Training Professional will often have to choose some form of external training supplier. This will be a crucial decision and the next chapter offers some guidance on how to approach it.

14

Choosing a Training Supplier

Introduction

Increasingly these days, organisations are using a higher proportion of external providers for all sorts of services. Charles Handy (1989) talks about the *shamrock* organisation made up of three different types of people:

- the *core workers* who are employed by the organisation, who are usually well qualified professional, technical and managerial staff, who are essential to the organisation
- the *contractural fringe* consisting of individuals and organisations to whom work is contracted
- the *flexible labour force* which consists of part-time and temporary workers.

There has been a trend over recent years for organisations to reduce their core workforce and make increasing use of contractors and part-time/temporary workers. This trend has certainly been in evidence in the training world with many organisations cutting back their training departments, in some cases to just an administrative/managerial centre, with no or very few training deliverers permanently on the staff. Instead, external training providers are used to provide training services as and when they are needed.

The first type of external training provision is where trainers or training consultants are brought in to develop and/or deliver training in the organisation. Perhaps most commonly they are brought in on a short-term contract basis, but all sorts of different arrangements are emerging. For example, one major transport organisation now employs what it calls 'training associates' who are bought in on an annual contract with an agreed fixed daily rate and guarenteed a minimum level of work. Other organisations set up one-off contracts for particular jobs.

The first approach overcomes one of the problems associated with using contractors − where you gain a specialist in the particular training area, but often the contractor will have very limited knowledge of the organisation itself. The associates cover a wide range of specialisms, but also begin to build up a detailed working knowledge of the organisation. Whereas it is possible to gain knowledge of the tangible aspects of an organisation, such as the nature of their products and services, their financial situation, etc it is far more difficult for an outside contractor to gain an understanding of the culture and current concerns of the workforce. This may not matter too much if the contractors are providing practical services, eg printing and/or cleaning. However, it matters a great deal when they are providing a service such as training which depends so much on understanding both the needs and attitudes of the delegates and the organisation at that particular time, and in the context of both where the organisation is coming from and to where it is going.

The second type of external training provision is the open courses provided by many training suppliers. As the name suggests these are pre-arranged courses on specific topics (eg project management, interviewing skills, EU legislation), which are open to anyone, or at least anyone who has the ability to pay the fees. There is a wide range of such courses and they constitute the external *buy* option discussed in the previous chapter.

We shall look at how you set about choosing the right training supplier for each option:

- to develop and deliver a new course − the make option
- to provide an open course − the buy option.

Choosing a training supplier − the make option

The process is very similar to going out to tender for any service (eg a building contract, a secretarial contract) and follows these steps:

- Step 1 − choose five or six suitable training suppliers

- Step 2 — ask each of them to submit a written training proposal based on the training specification
- Step 3 — based on the training proposal, select a shortlist of two or three suppliers for interview and to make presentations
- Step 4 — follow up references (if required)
- Step 5 — based on the presentations, interviews and references, choose the supplier.

Some organisations may skip Steps 1 and 2 as they are able easily to identify two or three suitable suppliers. For very large contracts or where your knowledge of potential suppliers is more limited, it may be sensible to seek out a longlist of suppliers and make your first judgements based on written proposals, which is generally a less time-consuming exercise than interviewing a large number of prospective suppliers. Whether you start with Step 1 or Step 3 the training specification provides the vital information for suppliers to prepare their proposals. The more comprehensive and accurate the specification, the clearer the picture the potential training suppliers will get of what is required and therefore the better the proposals they will be able to provide. A good training specification will also avoid the client, whether it be the internal Training Professional or the line manager, having to spend a lot of their time answering questions and generally providing information. A good training specification is a very efficient means of communication between the client and potential contractors.

Step 1 Choosing the longlist

So how do you choose your five or six potential training suppliers? There is no one answer to this, but various possible sources of advice are as follows:

- The Institute of Personnel Management (IPM) has a register of approved consultants for all types of personnel work, including training consultants. Consultants on this register must be IPM members and be able to supply detailed references from organisations for which they have worked.

- The local Training and Enterprise Councils (TECs) also have a register of what they call TECassured consultants, which will include training providers. They use a similar system as that employed by the IPM where detailed references are taken up. The register is primarily intended for use for TEC-funded or part-funded work.
- Various large registers of management consultants, eg Management Consultancy Information Service, Management Consultants' Association, can be referred to.
- Word of mouth from fellow Training Professionals can be a very valuable source of information.
- Scanning the professional journals, not just for adverts but also for articles on particular training programmes or general training issues may provide some useful reference points.
- For longer contracts or those involving considerable costs, advertising for suppliers may be the appropriate option. Public sector organisations also need to bear in mind the requirement to advertise in the European Union for contracts over a certain value.

Step 2 Assessing the written proposal

Use the following as a checklist — you should look for:

- a well-written and presented document — concise, well structured and easy to follow
- a clear description of how the supplier will meet the criteria of the specification, particularly the training objectives — this could be in the form of an outline programme — look at coverage and balance
- details of training methods — whether they are appropriate to the subject area and target training population
- details of the trainers to be used, including:
  - relevant qualifications and/or practical experience in the subject area
  - experience of training similar courses
  - experience of training similar types of delegate
  - experience of training in your organisation or similar organisations

- a timetable for the work involved − this is a good indicator of a professional and organised approach
- a breakdown of the costs − it goes without saying that cheapest is not always best − you need to be clear what you are getting for your money!

Using a checklist of this nature, it is usually not too difficult to pick out a shortlist of two or three suppliers. Just a couple of final points − beware the glossy brochure which tells you very little and the untidy, but lengthy and apparently very detailed theoretical treatise on the subject area of interest. Both are superficially beguiling − the first because the authors appear to be professional and well established, and the second because it is always tempting to get in the experts, but remember you also need people that can develop and deliver training in an organised way. It should be possible to get the right mixture of training professionalism and subject expertise − do not be tempted to trade off one for the other.

Step 3 Assessing a presentation/interview on a training proposal

When making the arrangements to interview the shortlist of suppliers ensure:

- that sufficient time is scheduled − there must be time for the issues to be probed
- the supplier are told how much time is available and if a formal presentation is required, given a time limit for the presentation itself
- all the relevant people can attend − it is often helpful to have a subject specialist available and a representative manager of the prospective delegates.

If a presentation is involved, and this is generally a sensible approach, assess the quality of the presentation, looking out for:

- a good opening, which grabs your attention and signposts the content (if they can't grab your attention at this stage, you may well wonder at their ability to hold the delegates' attention!)
- a good structure, with all the relevant areas covered in a clear and logical manner
- competent delivery
- a good close – with sensible summary and clear conclusions
- professional handling of questions.

Issues to probe, and again you can use the following as headings for a checklist, are:

- What is the content of the programme – how will it meet the training objectives?
- How will the training methods proposed help the delegates achieve the learning objectives?
- Who will actually deliver the training? With large training organisations the presenters will not necessarily be the trainers for any/all of the courses.
- What is the knowledge and experience of all the staff who will be involved in the development and delivery of the training?
- What is their reputation inside your organisation, if they have worked before in the organisation?
- What is their reputation outside your organisation? Seek references from other organisations.
- What evaluation methods are to be used?
- Are they able to meet the timescale?
- What are the costs?

Do not be afraid to probe. We have attended interviews of this nature as potential training suppliers, where remarkably little probing has taken place and much of what we have said has been taken at face value. Remember that it is not unusual for people to embellish the truth or perhaps skirt round areas of weakness.

Finally, think about how the supplier will fit into the organisation. Would you feel comfortable working with them? How will they relate to the delegates? How will they relate to any specialists or senior managers involved in the training project? This is an important and difficult part of the assessment — you are not necessarily looking for organisational clones but successful training does depend on the chemistry between the training deliverers and the delegates. It sometimes can be a balance between people who will fit in and also be able to challenge existing norms.

Step 4 Follow up references

If a prospective supplier is one that is new to the organisation, it is essential to take up references with the same rigour as you would on a prospective employee. In the case where they have originated from the sort of registers discussed in Step 1 (eg IPM Consultants Register), this will probably not be necessary unless you want to follow up a particular area of concern. It is also worthwhile checking whether the consultant subscribes to any appropriate code of professional conduct.

Step 5 Choose your supplier

You are now at the stage when you can choose your supplier based on the evidence of a written proposal, a presentation, an interview and references. Try and make your decision as promptly as possible and let the unsuccessful suppliers know as soon as you can.

Just as in a job interview, remember the assessment is two way — the training suppliers will also be judging you and your organisation. Will the training project be professionally run? Is it an organisation they want to work with or be associated with? It will pay great dividends to the quality of the final training project if this two-way process is handled well.

So on to the next area — how to choose a provider for an open course.

Choosing a training supplier – the buy option

There are in fact two questions here – what is the right provider and what is the right training. The problem that usually confronts the buyer is the range of choice available. Occasionally with very specialist areas, the problem may be seeking out a suitable course. The criteria for making the decision are:

- how well the course meets the training needs of the delegate(s) in terms of content, ie how well it meets the delegates' training objectives
- the quality of the course
- the affordability of the course – there can be quite a range of fee levels
- the timing of the course – suitability in terms of both how soon the training can take place and whether the specific dates are convenient to the delegate/organisation
- the convenience of the location – a delegate in the north of England may not relish a course held on the south coast and, of course, it may imply increased time away from work and additional travel costs. Some course locations are more accessible than others.

The last three criteria are quite straightforward to assess – the first two are harder and to a large extent are linked. So, first, how do you find out about courses? There are again several approaches, among which are:

- Registers such as the National Training Index (NTI). This is a privately run company which, for an annual subscription, provides a register of training courses either in the form of a catalogue or on computer disk to organisations seeking open courses. There are no charges to the training suppliers for being listed. The Index is subdivided by subject area and provides a brief description of each course + dates + location + costs. In addition it provides all subscribers with appraisal forms, which they ask to be completed when delegates from subscribing organisations attend any courses listed on the Index. In this way they

build up a data bank of assessment information on courses which is available free to subscribers. The NTI also provides assessments of training films and training venues.
- Specialist registers, eg LOGOS Directory of computer-based training products.
- Many of the larger training suppliers advertise widely – particularly in the personnel/training journals and, for specialist courses, in the relevant specialist journals as well as operating mailing lists. For example, the IPM publishes a guide to their 300+ training and development programmes.
- Local TECs keep current lists of training courses operating in their areas, on computer in local libraries.
- Professional institutes will be a source of information on professional training courses.

Having identified what appears to be a suitable course, seek as much detail as possible:

- Examine the content.
- Look critically at the training objectives – whether they meet the criteria set out in Chapter 12 and how closely they match the training objectives in the training specification.
- Assess the training methods.
- Press for evaluation data, most courses should be assessed at least by 'happy sheets' – examine the results, ask to see the questionnaire and judge its worth for yourself.
- Ask for names of recent delegates who can be approached to talk about the course.
- If you are proposing to send a large number of delegates, seek the opportunity to sit in on a course free of charge.

When you use open courses make sure you get feedback. Consider setting up your own evaluation system (see Section 6) based on your delegates' feedback and perhaps start a database of your own. When you get unsatisfactory feedback, report the comments back to the supplier – it is important that they have the opportunity to consider what may have been the cause and the opportunity to put it right. You will receive an excellent insight into the quality of the supplier by the way they handle what is effectively a customer complaint.

Conclusion

So where are we now? We have taken the identified training need and examined whether formal or informal training solutions would be appropriate. We have looked at the key exercise of preparing a training specification. We then went on to look at the make or buy options and finally how to choose training suppliers.

The next stage, set out in Section 5, Planning the Training, looks at the very important issue of welding the many separate training initiatives into a training plan and budget.

Section 5
Planning the Training

Introduction

In terms of the Training Wheel, we have gone round the stages of:

- identifying the range and extent of training needs from business needs (Sections 1 and 2)
- specifying those training needs very precisely (Section 3)
- analysing how best the training needs can be met (Section 4).

Having been very hard working, professional and systematic, the Training Professional is now in possession of a vast amount of data/information on business needs and the associated training needs at the organisational, departmental and individual levels. The problem now is how to plan and organise to meet those needs!

This section looks at this very important but sometimes neglected stage in the training process. Strictly speaking, purists might argue that this was not part of the training needs analysis stage. However, equally it tends not to be addressed in books on the development and delivery of training which concentrate more on the development, planning and delivery of specific individual courses. It is not an easy part of the process to discuss, largely because the preceding stages, ie getting at the training needs, can vary tremendously between different organisations and rarely fits the ideal of a well-ordered approach. Also, we live in a business world characterised by an ever-increasing pace of change.

It is rare for the Training Professional to be able, say, to assemble all the information on training needs during a specific period preceding the planning year, then formulate a training plan and budget. With limited resources it is likely that once the Training Professional has brought together all the bids for training, there will be the need for some considerable adjustment. It may even be as dramatic as revisiting the TNA process as a whole and re-asking all the questions previously posed. Through the iterative (and reiterative) process a final balance of what training can be achieved within the resources available will be arrived at. However, the process does not stop there. Training needs are often generated at short notice and needs and priorities can change all the time. So, it is important to be flexible and develop the ability to be able to respond and revise plans. In some organisations the training plan may have to be revisited regularly and adjusted.

However, this does not obviate the need for planning, rather it means that the Training Professional has to be both skilled in the planning process and willing and able to react to change. This section looks at:

- assembling and prioritising the information on training needs (Chapter 15)
- preparation and use of training plans (Chapter 16).

It does not purport to offer all the answers on this complex subject but tries to provide the basis for Training Professionals to develop an approach that best meets the needs and challenges of their own organisation.

Figure 5.1 shows where Section 5, Planning the Training, fits into the Training Wheel.

Figure 5.1

The Training Wheel — Planning the training

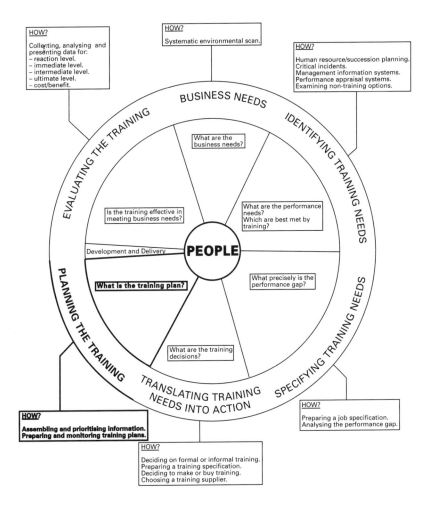

15

Assembling and Prioritising the Information

Introduction

In this chapter we look at how we assemble the information that has been so painstakingly gathered as part of the TNA process and how we prioritise it. It is the crucial first step in the preparation of the training plan and budget.

Assembling the information

The TNA process will have generated needs from a number of sources. In Section 2, Identifying Training Needs, we set out a range of what we described as windows into the business needs. These were:

- human resource planning
- succession planning
- critical incidents
- management information systems
- performance appraisal systems.

These basically generate information on the need for some sort of performance change in the human resources of the business – which might be for new skills and knowledge or an improvement in existing knowledge and skills being used. Having considered a range of ways that these performance changes can be achieved, training will be identified as the best approach in some cases. In those cases, the next stage will be to specify the training need very precisely to ensure that the training is focused and targeted to meet the business need in a cost-effective way (see Section 3, Specifying Training

Needs). Then each training need will be analysed to decide the best approach to meeting that need, be it informal or formal training, the appropriate training methods, etc. We suggested that the final output of this process should be some form of written statement detailing the training required — what we call a training specification.

At the simplest end of the spectrum, the TNA process can be seen to generate a mass of training specifications all posing demands on the training resources. At the other end of the spectrum, at its most chaotic, the TNA process can be seen to generate a mass of demands which are for the large part badly researched and poorly specified. Clearly, the closer you are to the ordered end of the spectrum, the easier life becomes at the planning stage.

Most people who live in the real world will know that they are unable to do all the things they might want to do. For the Training Professional the limiting factor is usually the availability (or rather, the lack) of money to finance the training. Other factors may be the lack of suitably qualified trainers or training accommodation or the operational constraints on the release of trainees. Whatever the reason it is clear that some prioritising will be necessary in the development of most training plans.

Setting priorities

Setting priorities will help you to decide:

- what training should be included
- in what order the training should be carried out
- what training might be put on a waiting list to be carried out in the event of some other training being cancelled or postponed
- what training might be left undone, with an assessment of the cost/effect of this decision.

Key information

The assembled data/information on training needs represents the shopping list for the Training Professional to work on. The key elements of the information which will aid the decision-making process are:

- details of the business need that the training is meeting
- the resources required in terms of finance, trainer/instructor time, delegate time, accommodation, etc
- the timescale(s) over which the training must take place.

All the above data/information would be contained in the training specification (see Chapter 12) and in the analysis of make or buy decision (see Chapter 13) for each item of training required. This documentation really comes into its own at this stage − it is clearly a key source of data for feeding into the prioritisation process.

The first stage is for the information on requirements to be compared with the resources that are available. For example in financial terms, if the training budget is set at a given figure and the anticipated total cost of all the proposed training needs is double that figure, then something has to give! Either the budget is increased to take account of all the specified training or some of the training bids have to be cut out or postponed. In reality the latter is more likely to be the case; however, we would argue that a well-thought out case on training to meet a specific business need could stand its ground against any other business proposal requiring budgeted funds.

Next some sort of assessment should be made against the other resources, eg accommodation and trainer availability. Both of these items lend themselves to being set out diagrammatically using PERT and Gantt charts. Examples of the use of these are given in Chapter 16 which looks at training plans. These techniques help to programme and schedule the timing of the training in order to get the most from the limited resources. As with many such tasks, there is a range of computer programs to help with the donkey work if the process is large or complex.

Key factors in prioritising

The key factors that might be considered when prioritising are:

- *Importance* – how big an impact will the completed training have on organisational performance, ie how important is the business need? The degree of importance could be affected by operational constraints, legal implications or by the return demonstrated in your cost/benefit analysis (see Chapter 22). Alternatively it could be the high visibility of the training or political factors that dictate decisions about relative importance. It may be helpful to give a high importance, medium importance or low importance ranking to the training bids. For example, in our second human resource planning case study, the Expanding Railway Company (p 27) there is a substantial increased demand for drivers in particular years. As there is no other source of supply other than training them internally and their presence is crucial to the planned expansion, this would merit a high ranking. It is important to remember, of course, that this is a very subjective process and might best be carried out by the Training Professional in conjunction with line manager colleagues. Some organisations actually set up groups or committees to make these sorts of decisions. It is important also to note that the rankings are relative. In giving a bid a low importance ranking is not to say it is unimportant but that it is less important than the other bids against which it is being judged.

- *Urgency* – how quickly must you act? Training is urgent if failure to complete it within a short timescale will have a high negative impact on the business and/or reduce or cancel the benefit of doing it. It may be helpful to use a concept drawn from the project planning technique, critical path analysis, of identifying the window of time over which the training must take place. With this technique, the earliest date that the training can be undertaken is identified, for example, if it is training for a new computer system it would be ineffective to carry out the training too soon. Then the latest date for the training is identified, for example, the training must be completed before the new computer system becomes operational. In the case of the drivers in the Expanding Railway Company, there will certainly be a latest date by which training must have been completed to meet the operational requirements of the expansion. There may be some flexibility in the earliest date if the additional drivers can regularly practise their skills before taking up their jobs, perhaps by covering for illness or double running. Some training may just come labelled highly urgent − to be done as soon as possible, for example, the training needs relating to health and safety such as arising out of the Awful Accidents case study (p 42). Some training, too, is highly constrained in terms of timescales for operational reasons. For example, retailers would not consider training any of their shop-floor staff in the run-up to Christmas and universities might elect to train their lecturing staff only in the student vacation periods.

- *Trend* − what happens if you do nothing? Will the business need stay the same or get worse? Or is it possible that the business need will reduce or actually go away, perhaps as staff learn on-the-job?

Your training plan (discussed in detail in Chapter 15) will now depend on the prioritising process of weighing up all the items on your list of training bids. If several training issues are of high importance, deciding which to put in the schedule first will depend on their relative urgency and trend. Thus the highly important, highly urgent training issues with a high trend to deteriorate without the training intervention would be prioritised first on the programme, with others taking their relative position. However, there is no easy way or simple algorithm to use. In general bids labelled high importance take precedence over bids ranked as medium and low, but it may be a matter of judgement to weigh up a medium importance bid with a high urgency rating against a high importance bid but where there is some flexibility in the timescale. For example, where the introduction of a new computer system could be delayed a couple of months, the training need could be pushed into the following budget year. Life is made a good deal easier if the planning can take place over a longer timescale than a year, even if it is accepted that for the later years the plan is tentative rather than firm.

Conclusion

In most organisations there will almost always be more bids for training than the financial and/or physical resources will allow. Following a systematic process such as that outlined above will help ensure that limited training resources are prioritised into those areas where they can have the biggest impact.

The process described above is not meant to be prescriptive for all organisations. Clearly local issues will be important in prioritising which training activities get the first call on resources – it is the setting up of the process, ie starting to think about the issues involved that is more important, not what the prioritisation process actually contains. Prioritising the training is, in our view, an essential step in the process and one which is often given scant attention, which means that it sometimes happens by default and is sometimes approached in a haphazard manner.

Who knows, at some stage in the future (or possibly in enlightened organisations even now) setting the training budget might be based on the training programme that is identified as delivering business success. This would be a significant improvement over the present situation in many organisations where the training budget is a fixed sum to be worked within – more about this vital subject in the next chapter.

16

Training Plans

Introduction

As we have found so often in previous sections it is important to start off by defining our terms. The term *training plan* is used in many different ways and to describe many different entities. It is interesting that the government survey, *Skills Needs in Britain* (Employment Department, 1993), found that 63 per cent of organisations (with 25+ employees) claimed they had what they called training plans, but only in 43 per cent of organisations did they exist as formal written statements!

We shall define the training plan as a composite document consisting of three parts:

- *a statement of policy* or direction for the period in question
- a *training budget* setting out the financial implications of the proposed programme of training
- an *operational plan* scheduling the training in terms of timing, resources used, eg trainers, accommodation, etc.

Traditionally training plans cover a period of a year. Some organisations may work on shorter periods such as six months and a few use longer periods, although in our experience this is unusual. As we commented in the previous section it can be very useful to plan over a longer period. Many of the methods of identifying training needs, eg human resource and succession plans, by their very nature will throw up needs over a considerably longer timescale than a year. Also, during the prioritising process, having the flexibility to plan further ahead can ease the situation where constraints are biting hard. A common complaint made about British management is the tendency towards short-termism. Investing in the human resource asset of a business must be a long-term strategy, so it makes sense to reflect this in the planning process.

We will look at each of the three sections of the training plan in turn.

Policy and direction

This section sets out any underlying policy themes that have either driven the training plan or are reflected by the prioritising process that has been used to decide on the training programme. Examples of policy themes could be:

- a move towards qualification training, perhaps setting targets for NVQs/SVQs
- a greater use of informal training methods, eg coaching on the job
- an emphasis on a specific form of training, eg interpersonal skills training rather than technical/professional skills
- the inclusion of a major training initiative, eg the training of all supervisors in leadership skills or an organisation-wide customer care initiative.

Such a section of the plan would normally also include comments on the overall budget for the period and trends, eg the percentage increase/decrease on the previous period, distribution between departments, type of training.

The training budget

It may be surprising to those Training Professionals who are used to working with training budgets to find that only just over half, 55 per cent, of medium and large organisations (25 + employees) have a training budget and in fact in less than half, only 45 per cent, it exists as a formal written statement (Employment Department, 1993). There are clearly considerable advantages to having an identified and dedicated source of funding for training. It implies a commitment to training and guarantees a certain level of training. Where a training budget does exist, it can take many forms these days. There has been a proliferation in the ways that organisations fund their training, often in response to a general policy of tightening the controls on the use of resources and increasing accountability for expenditure.

Who funds the training?

Newby (1992, p 217) debates whether training is best charged as an overhead across all other functions, according to some indicator such as number of staff employed, or whether it should be re-charged according to specific training provided to each function, with the training function operating as a form of profit centre. He suggests that there are advantages and disadvantages with both methods.

Newby argues that *overhead systems* encourage a longer term view of training with less emphasis on short-term fire-fighting. However, they tend to encourage the inertia of running a standard menu of courses from year to year with little attempt to review training provision against business needs. Also, they do not encourage line management to take an interest in the systematic identification of training needs, based on business needs, with the associated analysis and evaluation.

Re-charging systems, on the other hand, do have the virtue of concentrating line management interest on selecting the right people for the right training as they are being charged for the training used. Newby says that this alone is sufficient, in his view, to justify re-charging as opposed to overhead systems which leave line managers largely indifferent to the costs (and therefore benefits) of training. This is a view with which we strongly concur.

In our researches for this book we have found that there is no single trend of moving to one system or the other. Some organisations are moving towards re-charging while others are moving back to the overhead system. An example of this is a major financial institution which, prior to its take-over by another major financial organisation, used the re-charging system. The new owners have a policy that all the work and costs associated with internal re-charging (including for training) is simply not worth the effort, so they moved back to the overhead system of charging. Some organisations have taken re-charging one stage further with their separate business units holding their own training budgets. The training function has been set up as a self-financing business unit with a profit target. Each business unit, eg a particular product area, sets its own budgets and is able to purchase their training from any source — using resources internal to the business, from the internal training business unit or from any external supplier.

Another disadvantage of the overhead system is that it often leads to the training budget being determined by adding (or subtracting) a percentage to the actual spend on training in the previous financial period. This, in part, is responsible for the spurt in training in those organisations in the final quarter of their financial year! However, Newby comments that some organisations have overcome this by combining an overhead system with a system of zero-based budgeting. Here, in theory, each budget-setting exercise starts effectively with a clean piece of paper, no expenditure, and is built up from justified proposals.

Accounting for costs

It is not our intention, nor could we hope to do justice to it, to provide a detailed exposition of accounting principles and processes. How involved or knowledgeable the Training Professional will need to be will depend largely on the form of funding model used. The process will range at its simplest between monitoring expenditure against a sum of money to, at its most complex, the use of what are called absorption costing and marginal costing techniques.

Davies (1990, p 80) describes *absorption costing* in the following way:

> Absorption costing, or total costing, as it is sometimes called, helps to ensure that organisational costs are fully recovered when a price is quoted for a job or unit of consultancy.

Absorption costing is used in the case of training profit centres to ensure that the full costs of the training are recovered. There are the direct costs or variable costs, which can be directly attributable to a specific training session, eg the costs of the trainer, hire of facilities, costs of handouts, etc and the indirect costs or overhead costs, eg salaries of administrative staff, costs of office accommodation (accounted for by depreciation), development costs, etc. Absorption costing is a method used to allocate these overhead costs to individual training programmes and thereby arrive at the total costs of each programme. In Chapter 22, when we look at assessing the cost/benefit of training it will be important again to establish the total costs.

Marginal costing in very simple terms looks at the additional costs of an extra unit of activity. It assumes that the overhead costs have already been absorbed and that the marginal cost of the extra unit of activity, eg an extra session of an existing established course is only the direct/variable costs.

The overhead or fixed costs are likely to include:

- permanent accommodation, eg offices, training rooms, resource centre/library, taken into account through depreciation;
- permanent training equipment, fixtures and fittings, tables, desks, chairs, etc taken into account through depreciation
- standard charges for heating, lighting, rates, etc
- some administrative and management costs.

A type of fixed cost, but one which would be allocated over the life cycle of a training programme rather than over a particular period of time such as the financial year is, of course, the cost of training development. These costs would probably include:

- The salaries plus overheads of directly employed developers and/or the fees of consultants for this work. The elements of activity would be:
  - designing the form and structure of the training
  - designing the training material, eg where appropriate, case studies, role plays, games, models and mock-ups, videos and CBT material

- preparing pre-course material
- preparing handouts
- preparing evaluation tools.
- The cost of materials consumed during the development process.

Among the direct or variable costs (ie the costs that vary according to the volume of training delivered) are likely to be:

- costs of the trainers delivering the training − these may be the costs of consultants, guest speakers and/or salaries plus overheads and recruitment costs of internal training staff
- travel, residential and catering costs of delegates and trainers
- costs of duplicated training materials and handouts
- cost of licence fees for the use of copyright materials
- administrative costs involved in making arrangements for the particular course(s) and the delegates
- hire/maintenance of equipment and premises
- marginal costs of heating and lighting.

If you are calculating the total costs to the organisation of the training, for example when evaluating the training, then it will be necessary to include the costs of the delegates' time away from the workplace, either through a pro-rata time apportionment of their salary and associated costs or through the cost of replacements, stand-ins, overtime costs to make up lost time, etc.

Accounting for income

Where the training function is operating as a profit centre some form of budgeting for sales income will be required. The information on timings of revenue income would come from the operational plan scheduling the training (see page 165).

Contingency allowances

We have made no mention of the concept of the training budget including a contingency allowance for training arising from the business needs which could not be foreseen during the preparation of the budget. We would suggest that training focused on business needs has as much right to contingency funds as any other part of the organisation. The alternative, when a previously unforeseen need occurs, is to carry out a re-run of the prioritising exercise described in Chapter 15. Perhaps only when it can be demonstrated that no further slack can be shaken out of the budget, should there be made available any contingency or additional funds.

Monitoring and control of budgets

The monitoring and control of the training budget is an important activity. It is usually carried out at regular intervals, often monthly or in some cases quarterly. A comparison is made between the budget, ie the planned level of income and expenditure, and what has actually occurred. The key is to look for what are referred to as variances between the budget and the actual. Generally small differences are not of concern and quite often a form of tolerance limit is specified, perhaps + / − 5 per cent of the budget, and only variances outside this tolerance level are highlighted. If income is involved, it will be essential to know whether sales are on target and if not what action is required. Is it a timing problem, perhaps the training requirement has been delayed, and the income will occur in a later period? Or has the income been lost, in which case what effect will it have on the final outcome in terms of profit or loss for the budget period? If the variance arises on expenditure, it will be essential to find out what is the cause − is it a question of timing, or has there been a worrying increase in costs?

Another aspect of budgeting is for cash flow. Cash flow analysis is critical in running a commercial training enterprise where a shortfall of income against outgoings will require financing. Many businesses which are basically sound and profitable go under because of cash flow problems.

Costing and budgeting is often an area where the average Training Professional feels a little uncomfortable. The mechanics and approaches used will vary considerably between organisations. However, there are considerable benefits to understanding the concepts and systems involved. Our advice is not to be embarrassed to seek help and explanations from your financial colleagues. Setting up the training budget and monitoring it in a professional way will not only ensure that the training provision is securely and soundly based but will also ensure your credibility with both your financial and your line manager colleagues. You will be demonstrating that you appreciate the requirements for sound financial planning and stewardship!

Operational plans

The training budget is an excellent tool for planning and controlling the financial side of training. However, there is a need for operational plans scheduling the training in terms of timescale and non-financial resources. The operational plans will:

- set out the timescales for every stage of every training event, from preparation of the training specification if this is not already available, through the development stages of the training programme and its delivery and finally to the evaluation of the programme
- identify and schedule the resources required at all stages, for example:
  - your time
  - that of other trainers/instructors
  - accommodation
  - training materials
  - delegates' time (to ensure practicality of release).

Gantt charts

The most commonly used method for this type of planning is probably still the Gantt chart. Named after Henry Gantt, who first used horizontal bar charts for this purpose in the early 1900s (Young, 1993, p 55), the Gantt chart offers a method for setting out training activities in a straightforward, logical, diagrammatic form that is easy to understand. It can be used to plan and monitor the overall training programme or to plan and monitor a specific activity such as the development of a new training course to meet a specific business need. It can be used to show the training activities against a number of parameters although elapsed or calendar time is usually displayed along the base. Additional information such as key dates, review meetings, etc, can be shown with a variety of symbols and colours. A number of manual systems are used, such as peg boards and white boards, which enable it to be updated and modified relatively easily. Paper-based versions are often completed in pencil, again for ease of modification. There are also many computer packages which make the original drawing and any subsequent modification a quick and simple process. These also allow for the scheduling of resources to be carried out fairly effortlessly, whereas with manual systems this can be a laborious exercise. Such packages also allow for the monitoring of the plan to be undertaken very simply.

Gantt charts are not without their limitations. In particular it is not easy to show the relationship between the various training activities and therefore the knock-on effect of activities, eg the development of a training programme being accelerated or delayed, on other activities. Two techniques, critical path analysis (CPA) and the programme evaluation and review technique (PERT) were developed in the late 1950s to overcome this problem. The differences between the two project management techniques in practice has largely disappeared and the best features of both have been merged in modern computer packages. Not only do they enable the planning and scheduling process to take place effortlessly, but they will automatically adjust the whole programme for any changes made. These systems can provide the scheduling information in a wide variety of ways, including Gantt type charts.

An example of a Gantt chart is shown in Figure 5.2 (opposite). It sets out the schedule of training programmes

Figure 5.2
Example of a Gantt chart

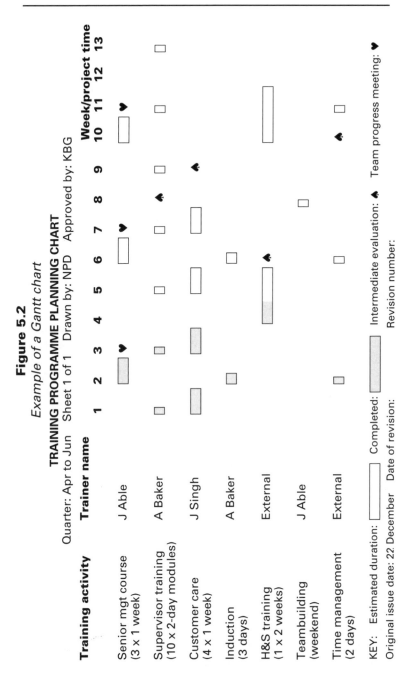

TRAINING PROGRAMME PLANNING CHART

Quarter: Apr to Jun   Sheet 1 of 1   Drawn by: NPD   Approved by: KBG

| Training activity | Trainer name | Week/project time |
| | | 1 | 2 | 3 | 4 | 5 | 6 | 7 | 8 | 9 | 10 | 11 | 12 | 13 |

KEY: Estimated duration: ☐   Completed: ▭   Intermediate evaluation: ◂   Team progress meeting: ❤
Original issue date: 22 December   Date of revision: Revision number:

167

to be undertaken over a particular period of time. You will see from Figure 5.2 that the chart has already taken into account the scheduling of the trainer resource so that there is no double-booking (hopefully!) of any trainer. Symbols can be used to show key dates but care should be taken to ensure that the chart does not become so cluttered that the detail is impossible to see. In our case we have limited ourselves to showing the timing and duration of the delivery of the courses, the team progress meeting (♥) following shortly after the training for a short course has been completed (and also midway through a long course), and the timing for the evaluation (♠) of those courses which are to be formally evaluated. We have used the term team progress meeting to cover whatever you want it to cover. For some organisations, this will be the time when the delegates get together with their line managers to discuss how the training went and how it will be applied. In other organisations it might mean a meeting of the trainers, with or without, the line managers to review how the training went and to make such adjustments as might be necessary to achieve the training objectives.

This is a very versatile planning tool. We could have a Gantt chart showing the planning of one training programme right through from the identification of the business need to the final evaluation or showing the activities/workload of a particular trainer or the use of a particular training facility, etc. Monitoring the training activity on the chart in Figure 5.2 can be shown by shading the bars on the chart to indicate activities having been completed or by drawing bars to represent the actual timing of activities underneath the planned activities to show any adjustment to the planned training or slippage from the plan.

Conclusion

We have looked at the three elements of a training plan. The training plan will not, of course, be *written in stone* but will be a working document against which decisions will be taken during the period, and reports made against training progress. It will almost certainly change over the period of its life, possibly many times. Any training plan needs to be monitored regularly, asking:

- Are you on plan and within budget?
- If not, what action is required, eg training to be rescheduled?
- Has anything new happened that might affect the plan, eg urgent, high priority new initiative?
- If so, how can the need be accommodated, eg any spare capacity, any possibility of additional budget, what existing training planned might be postponed?

Planning the training is a vital stage in ensuring that all the hard work that has gone into the TNA process is translated into effective action to meet the business needs. We now pass through the stage in the Training Wheel which deals with the detailed development and delivery of the training which is outside of the scope of this book and come to the final crucial stage — evaluating the training.

Section 6
Evaluating the Training

Introduction

There is a saying among pilots that a landing is not complete until you have walked away from the aircraft. The reason for this is that following the very demanding process of landing an aeroplane, it is all too easy for a pilot to relax and so during the relatively simple process of taxiing to a vacant space and parking the plane, to commit some enormous blunder. Something similar applies in the training field.

The Training Professional has taken a systematic approach to the identification and analysis of the training needs and the planning of the training. The training has been delivered to meet these needs and according to plan. It is very tempting at this stage to breathe a sigh of relief and file the papers away. However, we would argue that you have not yet walked away from the aircraft until you have evaluated the training. As with all aspects of a flight, the landing is best considered at the outset when planning the whole trip. Analogously, the evaluation of a training programme should be planned at the same time as the programme itself, ie during the TNA stage.

The starting point for this section must be to establish what in fact we mean by the evaluation of training. It is one of those words much bandied around and equally much misunderstood. Or rather, perhaps, it is a word that means different things to different people. For many Training Professionals it provokes a sense of fear − should they be doing some of it and a sense of panic − how should they be doing it? A good place to begin is with what could be described as the classic or textbook definition of training evaluation provided by the Manpower Services Commission (1981):

> The assessment of the total value of a training system, training course or programme in social as well as financial terms. Evaluation differs from validation in that it attempts to measure the overall cost benefit of the course or programme in social as well as financial terms.

Fear and panic setting in? Don't despair, take a deep breath and read on. It is recognised that this is a very ambitious definition and, we believe, a more useful and practical definition is that provided by Hamblin (1974):

> Any attempt to obtain information (feedback) on the effects of a training programme, and to assess the value of training in the light of that information.

Some might argue that this definition is too loose, too unspecific and suggests an undisciplined approach. However, we believe that evaluation is often not attempted because people think that evaluation involves large, sophisticated (and expensive!) studies. In fact, there are many ways to evaluate training − each provides some information or some window into the process − and we would argue that any attempt at evaluation is better than none at all. The purpose of this section is to introduce a structured way at look at evaluation and then discuss a range of tools and techniques that can be used in the evaluation process.

Purposes of evaluation

Training evaluation is carried out for a wide range of purposes, which can be categorised generally under four main headings:

- to improve the quality of the training − in terms of the delivery, eg trainer, methods, length of training, the training objectives − content, level
- to assess the effectiveness of − the overall course, trainer, training methods
- to justify the course − prove that the benefits outweigh the costs
- to justify the role of training − for budget purposes, in cutback situations.

Usually the evaluation will have one of these purposes as its primary focus. For example, if there has been a number of general complaints about a training programme, then the evaluation will be directed primarily at identifying the cause and improving the quality. If there are concerns that the training is not achieving what was intended, then the evaluation will start by looking at the effectiveness of the training. If there are concerns about the costs of the course or whether there is a cheaper way of achieving the same results, then it will focus first on justification. If the organisation has a tough budget-setting process or is looking for cutbacks, then the emphasis may be on providing proof that training justifies the investment in it. They are clearly all interlinked and to some extent any evaluation addresses all four purposes. However, being clear on the primary purpose will help focus the evaluation on the appropriate issues and determine the best approach from the outset.

The results from evaluation studies can also provide invaluable information on how effective the training has been in meeting individual delegates' needs. Hence, the results can be used to provide feedback to the individual delegates and identify whether and what further interventions might be required. In the same way, assessments that are set up primarily to assess the individual delegates, eg tests used as the basis for licensing an individual to do a job, can also be used to provide evaluation information on the effectiveness of the whole course.

Given all these purposes, many would be forgiven for wondering how it was possible to get away with *not* evaluating training. Surely, everyone wants to strive continuously for improved quality, surely everyone wants to assess the effectiveness of its product, staff and methods and, finally, surely you must have to prove that training represents a good investment? Yet the evidence suggests that the evaluation carried out is very limited. The *Training in Britain* survey (Training Agency, 1989) estimated that only 15 per cent of organisations tried to evaluate the benefits of training and only 2.5 per cent attempted cost/benefit analysis. In some ways it seems extraordinary that training appears to escape the normal quality and financial criteria. One of the costs of this has undoubtedly been to make training a soft target for budget cuts at times of financial stringency.

175

There is increasing recognition of the importance of evaluation. The government initiative Investors in People puts a heavy emphasis on the need for evaluation and quotes one of the four essential principles underpinning the scheme (Employment Department, 1991) as:

An Investor in People evaluates the investment in training and development to assess achievement and improve future effectiveness.

Just under a quarter of the indicators used for assessing an organisation for recognition as an Investor in People involve the evaluation of training.

We hope that we have convinced you of the need to read on!

Levels of evaluation

The traditional model for evaluation dates back to the late 1960s and the work of Kirkpatrick (1967) and Warr, Bird and Rackham (1970). This proposes four levels of evaluation:

- *reaction level* − which measures what the delegates *think* or *feel* about the training
- *immediate level* − which measures what the delegates *learned* from the course
- *intermediate level* − which measures the effect of the training on *job performance*
- *ultimate level* − which measures the effect on *organisational performance*.

Hamblin (1974) divides the fourth level into two − distinguishing between the effect on organisational objectives, such as sales, productivity, absence rates, etc and looking at the economic effects ie some form of cost/benefit analysis. In our experience most organisations work with the four levels but sometimes refer to them as Level 1 (reaction) to Level 4 (ultimate). For the purposes of this book we will use the levels as set out above, but like Hamblin tackle the assessment of cost/benefit separately. Chapter 17 provides the basic building blocks for the rest of the section in describing how to set about collecting the data. Chapters 18 to 21 address the issues of why and how to tackle evaluation at each of the evaluation levels. Chapter 22 considers the cost effectiveness and the cost/benefit of training. Chapter 23 provides a starting point for analysing evaluation results. It introduces some simple techniques and refers the reader to other sources of information for more sophisticated analyses. The final chapter, Chapter 24, looks at some of the issues associated with the presentation and use of evaluation results.

So now we begin our journey around the final segment of the Training Wheel (see Figure 6.1).

Figure 6.1
The Training Wheel – Evaluation

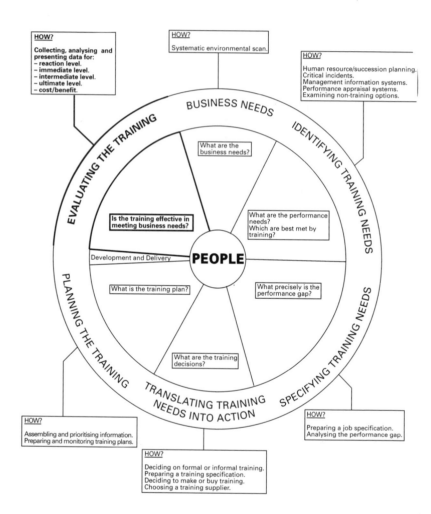

17

Collecting the Data

Introduction

How the data is collected is a key issue. The first vital stage in any data collection exercise is to *plan* it. You need to ask the questions:

- Why are you collecting the data? What is the purpose of the survey or data collection exercise? What are your objectives?
- Based on your objectives, what do you need to know? It is essential to be crystal clear about what information you need and in what form. It is also important not to be side-tracked into collecting information that might be useful or seems interesting! The downfall of many data collection exercises is that they get bogged down by attempts to collect too much data. It is crucial to remain focused on your objectives.

You then need to decide on:

- the design of the study itself
- methods of data collection
- issues of validity and reliability

This chapter looks at each of these areas in turn.

Design approaches to the evaluation study

There is a range of design approaches that may be taken to a particular evaluation study. The two simplest involve only the group being trained. These are:

- taking measurements *after* the training only and usually involves comparisons against some target of desired performance

- taking measurements *before* and *after* the training and assessing any gains in performance.

The first approach allows for checking that the training has achieved its objectives. However, without a starting level there is no way of assessing how much the training has contributed to the achievement of these objectives. Perhaps, all the delegates would have achieved similar results without the training! The second approach does allow for the measurement of the gain in performance as a result of the training. However, if this is a training programme spread over a period of time the delegates perhaps would have achieved this gain or a good part of it without training, just through experience on the job. This leads us on to the more sophisticated design approaches which involve the use of control groups.

Control groups are used as a method of trying to eliminate the effects of other factors which might influence the results of the evaluation. A control group is chosen to be as similar as possible to the study group, ie the group being trained. Both groups are assessed at the start. The study group receives the training, the control group does not and then both groups are assessed at the end. The gain in performance of the study group is then compared with the gain in performance of the control group. The difference in gain then should reflect the impact of the training over and above the other factors.

This approach is analogous to carrying out an experiment and these different approaches are referred to as *experimental designs*. These designs can become more complex. For example, there is evidence that merely being the recipient of attention in some form can have an effect on performance. In other words, simply being subject to the training (attention) may be causing some or all of the performance gain. This is often referred to as the Hawthorne effect (see Chapter 10, p 83). This effect is counteracted by giving the control group some sort of placebo, ie mimicking the attention given by training. Now using a placebo is a relatively simple concept, for example, in drug experiments where it can be a sugar pill looking and tasting just like the drug.

However, in the context of training evaluation experiments it is not nearly so easy. In some studies the placebo has been a form of team briefing. However, in this type of situation it is hard to find a placebo that would not have some sort of effect in its own right. One possibility is that the control group could be trained in an area totally unrelated to the performance needs being addressed by the training programme under study. To deal with this some more sophisticated designs introduce a second control group which is given the placebo, while the first remains subject to no action.

Yet a further complication is added if it is felt that the results are affected simply by taking the measurements at the start − then a third control group is added which is only assessed at the end. These designs can be illustrated diagrammatically, as shown in Figure 6.2.

In practice it is difficult to find control groups which are similar to the group being trained and the difficulty is clearly compounded if more than one control group is required. Most evaluation studies either use no control group or at most one, either with or without a placebo being introduced. However, understanding the purpose of the different designs helps understand the limitations of whatever design is chosen.

Methods of data collection

There are four main methods of collecting data (which are the same methods covered in Chapter 10, Investigating the Performance Gap):

- self-complete questionnaires
- interviews
- observation
- desk research.

Each method has its advantages and disadvantages which need to be taken into account when deciding on the best approach for collecting data for a particular evaluation purpose. We look briefly at each in turn.

Figure 6.2
Experimental designs

Measuring against a target performance:

training
————————   measure

Measuring changes in performance:

* no control group

  A   measure   training   B   measure

* one control group (non-training effects)

  A   measure   training   B   measure

  C   measure   no action   D   measure

* two control groups (Hawthorne effect)

  A   measure   training   B   measure

  C   measure   no action   D   measure

  E   measure   placebo   F   measure

* three control groups (pre-training measurement effect)

  A   measure   training   B   measure

  C   measure   no action   D   measure

  E   measure   placebo   F   measure

  G   no action   H   measure

Based on Whitelaw (1972)

Self-complete questionnaires

The advantages of self-complete questionnaires are that they:

- are a low-cost way to gather data
- can be a quick way to gather data

- make least demands on the time of the delegates/their managers
- involve no 'observer/interviewer' effects
- if carefully designed, provide results which can be readily analysed.

The disadvantages are:

- there can be low response rates which in turn can lead to biased responses, eg only those with a particular axe to grind will respond
- that to ensure as high a response rate as possible the questionnaire must be short and easy to complete, which generally means it must be highly structured, ie tick box options, with only a few questions allowing free or open comment
- this in turn limits the opportunity to probe the responses
- the questionnaires require very careful design to ensure clarity and lack of ambiguity.

This is a very common form of assessment and basically the evaluator trades depth of information either to get breadth of coverage or for reduced costs.

Interviews

There are three possible interview approaches available:

- the traditional face-to-face, one-to-one interview
- the telephone interview
- group interviews.

The traditional face-to-face, one-to-one interview has the following advantages:

- it ensures a response
- it enables responses to be clarified and probed
- it enables complex issues to be explored
- although it is important to plan and structure the interview, this is usually an easier process than designing a self-complete questionnaire.

The disadvantages are:

- it is relatively costly
- it requires skilled interviewers
- the involvement of an 'interviewer' can affect the results, ie interviewer bias
- it can be difficult to analyse.

The telephone interview can be considerably cheaper, but is a less sensitive tool and the quality of probing and exploration of issues is reduced. Group interviews are excellent for raising and discussing issues. They can provide powerful qualitative information on the training experience and are particularly good for clarifying problem areas and establishing causes of effective and ineffective training.

Observation

The one important advantage of this method is that:

- behaviour is being assessed directly.

The disadvantages are that:

- it can be costly as there is usually a minimum observer to delegate ratio of 1:1
- it can be a time-consuming approach
- the results can be influenced by the Hawthorne effect (see Chapter 10, page 83).

This is an important method of data collection in training evaluation, as training is very often directed at skills development.

Desk research

This involves making use of data that has already been collected for other purposes and therefore is sometimes referred to as secondary research. It is an important method of data collection for ultimate level evaluation where data on organisational performance will need to be monitored. It may also be used for other purposes, eg to make comparisons with other organisations, to take into account non-training effects on results such as economic conditions, etc. In addition, it covers activities such as reading up on evaluation studies carried out previously within the organisation and by other organisations. For example, the police keep a central register of evaluation studies carried out by the various county police forces.

The advantages are that:

- it is usually a low-cost method
- data can often be collected quickly.

The disadvantages are that:

- the data is not always in exactly the form that it is required and it is important to be aware of its limitations, eg does it cover all employees or only particular groups, how accurate and reliable is it?
- the data may be out of date
- the data may be difficult to access.

As with any method of data collection it is vital to plan how the data is to be collected. However with this method, since it does not usually involve the design of some sort of formal survey instrument such as a questionnaire, it is all too easy to leap straight in without a plan. This can lead to a considerable waste of time and even worse the wrong data being collected — so the message is plan and design your desk research in just the same way as you would any more formal survey.

Questionnaire design

Questionnaires in one guise or another feature in all the data collection methods:

- The self-complete questionnaire method requires a questionnaire that will stand on its own without the benefit of the further explanation that could be given by an interviewer or observer. It is usually highly structured.
- The interview method requires an interview form, which can range in format from a form that it is almost as highly structured as a self-complete questionnaire to one which just sets out the main areas or subject headings that need to be covered.
- The observation method requires an observation sheet to record the observed behaviour. These sheets can include questions ranging from simple yes/no statements to whether the particular behaviour or skill has been observed, noting the frequency of the behaviour occurring, through to rating the level of skill observed and making comments.
- The desk research method requires a recording plan which can vary from subject headings through to a detailed layout for the recording of the relevant data.

It is vital that the questionnaires are well designed. Questionnaires that are going to be used as formal survey instruments should go through the following stages:

- initial design
- pre-test — an informal trial, trying out the self-complete questionnaire or interview form, etc on a small group as similar to the target population as possible
- redesign as necessary
- pilot survey — a small scale test survey of the target population
- redesign as necessary
- full survey.

Appendix 17.1 at the end of this chapter provides a short introduction to questionnaire design, covering the types of questions that can be asked and some useful tips particularly directed at the design of self-complete questionnaires. It also provides suggestions for useful further reading.

Validity and reliability

There are three key aspects that need to be considered in any evaluation study:

- internal validity
- external validity
- reliability.

The *internal validity* of an evaluation study is concerned with how well the study measures what we want or are aiming to find out. This usually involves the adequacy and appropriateness of the measuring tool, the instrument, used. For example, if we are using a questionnaire, are the questions appropriately worded to elicit the information that is required? Does the knowledge test effectively measure the knowledge that has been learned from the training? Does the skills test include all the critical steps and are the measurement scales used appropriate? If we are measuring work performance, have we established the appropriate indicators? Approaches such as testing the instruments widely, using alternative approaches to measuring the same attribute all help toward establishing the internal validity of the study.

The *external validity* of an evaluation study is concerned with the extent that the findings can be applied beyond the group involved in the study. If a study has measured the effectiveness of a specific training course using 50 delegates from perhaps 200 delegates that had been on the training course, can the results be applied to the whole 200? Here we are entering the realms of sampling that go beyond this book. However, the answer is a tentative yes, subject to the sample of 50 delegates having been chosen appropriately (ie so that they represent the whole group) and acknowledging that any results are only estimates for the whole population and therefore that the actual result for the whole population lies somewhere in a range around the estimate. Sampling is quite a tricky area; some suggested further reading material is given at the end of Chapter 23 ('Further help'), or consider consulting a friendly statistician in your organisation.

On a wider scale, if a training programme has been assessed as effective in one area of the organisation, can you generalise the conclusions to the whole organisation? Again, it all depends on how similar the delegates are in their starting levels of knowledge and skills, their experience of the organisation, etc. If you demonstrate that one, two or three training programmes are effective, does this mean they all are? It depends! It is often very tempting to use results of evaluation studies beyond their original purpose – the message from this section is that you need to take care when you do so and be very clear what assumptions you are making when you do this.

The last issue that needs to be considered is that of *reliability*. The reliability of an evaluation study is the extent to which the results can be replicated, ie if the study was repeated the results would be the same. The obvious approach to dealing with this issue is to repeat tests and observations. Also techniques, such as including the same question but in different forms, using multiple observers, etc can be helpful.

This list of issues that need to be considered can sometimes sound rather daunting – how can you possibly design an evaluation study that passes all these tests? The answer is that in practice you cannot – what is important is that you are aware of the issues and that as far as is practicable you have designed and then used your study in as professional a way as is possible.

Conclusion

This chapter has introduced the issues concerned with the design of an evaluation study and discussed the different methods of collecting data. As some form of questionnaire is at the heart of all the data collection methods, the basic principles of questionnaire design are set out. Finally, the key issues of how valid and reliable are your evaluation results is covered. On now to tackling training evaluation at the first level – reaction level evaluation.

Appendix 17.1 Introduction to questionnaire design

Introduction

This appendix provides a brief introduction to questionnaire design and covers:

- the types of question that can be used
- some useful do's and don'ts for the design of question-naires, particularly the self-complete variety.

Types of questions

There are five main types of question:

- classification questions
- coded/structured questions
- open-ended questions
- semantic differential type questions
- Likert type questions.

We will look at each of these types of question in turn.

Classification questions

Purpose:

- for analysis of the data
- to check the representativeness of a sample.

Examples:

- age
- sex
- grade
- occupation
- department.

Coded/structured questions

The respondent is given a limited choice of answers.

Purpose:

- to test knowledge
- to establish facts
- to measure attitudes.

Examples:

How long must an employee have been employed before s/he can bring a claim for unfair dismissal on the grounds of race or sex? Please tick the appropriate box:

One year ☐
Two years ☐
No time limit ☐
Don't know ☐

Please indicate the five most important purposes of team briefings. Please put a **1** against the most important, a **2** against the next most important, and so on.

Give information on objectives/targets ☐
Receive information/feedback ☐
Discuss company issues ☐
Discuss job issues ☐
   etc
Other, please describe:_____

Advantages:

- quick and easy to complete
- easy to analyse.

Disadvantages:

- hard to design
- forces choice, may cause bias.

Open-ended questions

The respondent is free to give any answer.

Purpose:

● to test knowledge, usually of more complex areas/issues
● to measure attitudes.

Examples:

What information should be included in the record of...?
Describe what you would do if...
What do you think about the new proposals for...?

Advantages:

● gives no hints to the answers
● allows free expression of attitudes
● no bias
● easy to design.

Disadvantages:

● difficult to analyse
● requires a strong marking frame, ie, a framework for assessing the answers in the case of knowledge tests and coding and categorising schemes for attitude and opinion information.

Semantic differential type questions

The respondent is asked to assess something on a seven point scale. Other number scales can be used.

Purpose:

● to assess skills
● to measure attitudes.

Examples:

Please assess the chairmanship skills of the delegate, by circling the appropriate rating:

Strong control   1 2 3 4 5 6 7   Weak control
Listened well   1 2 3 4 5 6 7   Did not listen

What are your views on bullying in the workplace?
Very serious issue 1 2 3 4 5 6 7   Not a serious issue
Occurs frequently 1 2 3 4 5 6 7   Occurs not at all

Advantages:

- allows for a structured range of responses
- easy to analyse.

Disadvantages:

- subjective judgements on rating scale.

Some issues:

- whether or not to be consistent with which is the favourable extreme, ie left or right
- whether to have a middle option, ie use an odd number scale (eg 5, 7, 9), or whether to use an even number scale to force a choice between the top half and the bottom half of the scale and avoid respondents' tendency to go for the middle option.

Likert type questions-

The respondent is asked to indicate his/her views against a rating which is specified.

Purpose:

- to assess skills
- to measure attitudes.

Examples:
Please indicate your views on the new disciplinary procedures, by ticking the appropriate box:

	Strongly agree	Agree	Not sure	Disagree	Strongly disagree
Easy to understand	☐	☐	☐	☐	☐
Will improve discipline *etc*	☐	☐	☐	☐	☐

Please assess the chairmanship skills of the delegate, by ticking the appropriate box:

	Poor	Fair	Good	Very good
Control of meeting	☐	☐	☐	☐
Listening skills *etc*	☐	☐	☐	☐

Advantages:

- allows for a structured range of responses
- specifies the meaning of the scale.

Disadvantages:

- constrains response
- can cause bias.

Some issues:

- important to have a balanced set of response options
- whether to have a middle option (for the same reasons as listed for the semantic differential type question).

Dos and don'ts of questionnaire design (Self-complete questionnaires)

- keep questionnaire as short as possible
- keep questions as short and simple as possible
- use simple language – avoid technical/jargon words or acronyms, eg:
    How many special incidents have you been involved in?
    How many DP forms are there?
    Do you use DCF techniques?
- avoid questions which rely heavily on memory – use the appropriate time span, eg:
    How many training courses have you been on in the last five years? (Can you remember how many training courses you have been on in the last five years? A year may be the more appropriate time span.)
    How many times have you used the staff restaurant in the last six months? (One month might be more appropriate.)
- avoid ambiguous questions, eg:
    How many employees are you responsible for? (What does 'responsible for' mean – the employees that directly work for you, all the employees in the department that you head, those that you are professionally responsible for?
    Do you have a computer? (What does have mean – at home or at work, for your sole use or access to, etc?)
- avoid leading questions and using emotive words, eg:
    Do you feel that your manager should be more supportive?
    Do you think the company should forbid the use of telephones for personal calls?
- avoid multiple questions, eg:
    Do you think the company need more and better training?

- avoid double negatives

    Please indicate whether you agree or disagree with the
    following statement:

    Managers should not be required to record their time
    on duty.

    Agree
    Disagree

- avoid 'presuming' questions, eg:

    How many training specifications have you prepared in
    the last six months? (This should be preceded by a
    filter question − have you prepared ... ?)

- questions should always be able to stand alone, eg:

    How old was your baby when it arrived? (This was
    made clear by the previous question − when did you
    receive your free sample of milk!)

- try to avoid hypothetical questions − you will get a
  hypothetical answer!

    Would you use a physiotherapist at work if one was
    available? (It is more productive to probe experience,
    eg of using a physiotherapist).

- if you are providing a structured list of choices, always
  give a Don't know, Not applicable, Other, Please specify
  option

- PAY ATTENTION TO DETAIL, eg:

    Instructions for completing the questionnaire or in-
    dividual questions

    - tick one box only
    - routing or skip-to instructions − if Yes, go to
      Q6 ...
    - contiguous, not overlapping categories − age
      21−25, 26−30, 31−35, *not* 21−25, 25−30,
      30−35.

Suggested further reading

For a good all-round introduction to questionnaire design try
Oppenheim (1992). For an easy-to-read, lively guide primarily to the structuring and wording of questions and some
pitfalls to avoid, try Converse and Presser (1986).

18

Reaction Level Evaluation

Introduction

Reaction level evaluation basically answers the question of whether the delegates were happy or satisfied with the training. It is the delegates' own views or reactions to the training process that they have just experienced. Most organisations carry out some form of reaction level evaluation. There is considerable scepticism about the usefulness of this type of evaluation and the questionnaires used are often referred to somewhat derogatorily as *happy sheets*. However, it does measure an important aspect of training effectiveness − the satisfaction of at least one of the customers for the training, the delegate. Although we have found no studies that link good reaction level results to improvements in job performance, intuitively it would seem likely that if a delegate is satisfied or happy with the training there will be a willingness to transfer any learning back to the job. On a very practical level, the delegates will have the most relevant views on the venue, catering and administration. In addition, reaction level evaluation provides a relatively straightforward and low-cost source of evaluation information.

However, reaction level evaluation provides only part of the picture. It does not provide any objective assessment of whether training objectives have been met nor what the gain in learning has been, nor of how job performance has been affected. Apart from the uses set out above, it becomes most valuable when problems are identified through the other levels of evaluation and it can provide a basis for starting to analyse what has gone wrong.

How do we do it?

This form of evaluation is normally undertaken using a self-complete questionnaire. The questionnaire is usually highly

structured, ie the delegate has to choose between a range of options, with one or two general open questions at the end. Such questionnaires are not hard to design and usually cover the areas of:

- the existence/adequacy or pre-course briefing
- the extent to which delegates *feel* that the learning objectives of the course have been met
- the trainer's performance
- the training methods used
- the venue − its location, quality of facilities and catering
- the quality of the administration.

The length and detail of the questionnaire will depend on the nature of the course and the type of delegates. Some examples of reaction level questionnaires are provided in the Appendices at the end of this chapter. Appendix 18.1 is a detailed questionnaire and might be most useful for management training courses. Appendix 18.2 might be used for short courses, or for technical and basic vocational training, where a simpler questionnaire might be appropriate.

The evaluation is usually carried out at the end of a course, although it can be carried out at the end of various stages of the course, eg at the end of each day, or at the end of specific sections of the training. If a course is longer than a week, it is sensible to seek delegates' reactions at the end of the discrete parts, such as modules. If a course is being piloted, then it may be useful (subject to delegate fatigue!) to complete questionnaires at the end of each session.

Some key issues

Two key issues are:

- Should the questionnaire be completed during the course, rather than delegates taking the questionnaire away and completing it away from the course environment?
- Should the questionnaire be anonymous?

The first is a much debated issue. There is little doubt that the traditional approach of completing these questionnaires in the last half hour of a course causes a number of problems:

- the delegates may not have had time to reflect on the issues being raised by the questionnaire
- the delegates may be tired (and keen to get off home!)
- the delegates may be influenced by the group view
- the delegates may be too aware of the presence of the trainer and this may inhibit honest responses.

An alternative approach is to ask the delegates to complete the questionnaire after the course and return it. This overcomes most of the above problems. However, many organisations try this approach and then find that it founders on the difficulty of getting the questionnaires returned, which either results in low response rates or considerable administrative effort to ensure a decent level of return.

In practice, the best approach is probably to complete the questionnaires during the course, but to follow some simple guidelines:

- introduce and hand out the questionnaires at the beginning of the course, so that delegates can reflect on the questions during the course
- schedule time for completion of the questionnaires in the programme
- emphasise that the purpose of the questionnaires is to ensure that the training is meeting their needs and to monitor and improve quality
- brief the trainers on how to introduce and administer the questionnaires.

The second issue is anonymity. Again there are pros and cons. Clearly, delegates may feel more able to give honest feedback if they cannot be identified. This particularly may be the case in small organisations using internal trainers, who are seen as colleagues. With the use of good classification questions, anonymity should not pose any problems for the analysis. The major drawback is that responses cannot be followed up. So, for example, if some delegates rate some aspect of the course, or the whole of it, as poor, it is not possible to go back and find out more details. Also, from a customer care perspective there are considerable benefits to following up your dissatisfied customers.

Some useful approaches

The other important 'reactions' that it might be helpful to monitor at this stage are those of the other key players in the process – the trainers. They will probably provide the best insight into why certain training objectives might not have been met – perhaps, because of the starting levels of knowledge and skills of that particular group or because it became apparent that they were not relevant or less relevant than some other areas of the training. Their comments on the general content, level, length of the course and training methods used may be particularly useful in the early stages of a training programme's life. As with the delegates, the trainers' views on the practical aspects of the programme, eg quality of training facilities, are particularly relevant. An example of a trainer feedback form is provided as Appendix 18.3. Some organisations use these, but their use is not as widespread as might be expected given what a simple and cheap form of information they provide.

Conclusion

As mentioned earlier, this level of evaluation can provide lots of information at a relatively low cost. Once they have been designed (and organisations mostly use a couple of standard questionnaires which are then only customised in a minor way – perhaps to make changes to the training objectives), the data collection is free in that the forms are usually administered and collected by the trainers. The approach of generic questionnaires has the double advantage that it cuts down the design costs and more importantly allows comparisons to be made easily between different training programmes. However,

199

reaction level evaluation does generate an enormous amount of data. Many organisations now design their questionnaires so that they can be scanned directly into a computer and analysed using specifically developed computer programs.

We shall go on now to look at the next level of evaluation — the immediate level.

Appendix 18.1   Reaction level questionnaire (detailed)

DELEGATE ASSESSMENT OF THE TRAINING PROGRAMME

Course title: _____   Course date: _____

Name: _____   Manager's name: _____

Job title: _____   Job title: _____

Department: _____

We want to ensure that the training you receive is of high quality and of relevance to your job. We would be grateful if you would complete this questionnaire as frankly and as fully as possible.

---

1. PRE-COURSE BRIEFING

Did you receive a pre-course briefing from your manager?   Yes ☐   No ☐

If Yes, please indicate the extent to which the briefing helped you prepare for the course by circling the appropriate rating (1 indicating of little or no help ... 6 indicating of great help).

Knowing what the learning objectives of the course were   1 2 3 4 5 6

Understanding why you were on the course   1 2 3 4 5 6

Understanding how the course related to your job   1 2 3 4 5 6

---

2. TRAINING OBJECTIVES

Please indicate the extent to which you feel the training objectives were met by circling the appropriate rating (1 indicating not met at all . . . 6 indicating fully met).

1. _____	1 2 3 4 5 6	
2. _____	1 2 3 4 5 6	
3. _____	1 2 3 4 5 6	
4. _____	1 2 3 4 5 6	
5. _____	1 2 3 4 5 6	
6. _____	1 2 3 4 5 6	

3. PRACTICAL RELEVANCE

Please indicate the practical relevance of the course to your job by circling the appropriate rating.

Not relevant 1 2 3 4 5 6 Very relevant

4. TRAINING METHODS

In the development of your understanding and skills, please comment on the usefulness of the following training methods. Please circle the appropriate rating (1 indicating of no use . . . 6 of great use) or the Not Used category.

Tutor input sessions	1 2 3 4 5 6	Not Used
Group discussions	1 2 3 4 5 6	Not Used
Case studies	1 2 3 4 5 6	Not Used
Role plays	1 2 3 4 5 6	Not Used
Practical exercises	1 2 3 4 5 6	Not Used
Videos	1 2 3 4 5 6	Not Used
Handouts	1 2 3 4 5 6	Not Used
Other _____	1 2 3 4 5 6	

5. TRAINER(S)

In the development of your understanding and skills, please comment on the quality of your trainer(s) by circling the appropriate rating (1 indicating low quality . . . 6 high quality).

Lead Trainer

Appropriate pace	1	2	3	4	5	6
Knowledgeable	1	2	3	4	5	6
Creating interest	1	2	3	4	5	6
Involving the group	1	2	3	4	5	6

Second Trainer

Appropriate pace	1	2	3	4	5	6
Knowledgeable	1	2	3	4	5	6
Creating interest	1	2	3	4	5	6
Involving the group	1	2	3	4	5	6

Other Speakers/Trainers

_____	1	2	3	4	5	6
_____	1	2	3	4	5	6

6. FACILITIES AND ADMINISTRATION

Please indicate your satisfaction with the quality of the facilities and administration by circling the appropriate rating (1 indicating low quality . . . 6 indicating high quality) or the Not Used category.

FACILITIES:

Training room(s)	1	2	3	4	5	6	Not Used
Bedrooms	1	2	3	4	5	6	Not Used
Catering	1	2	3	4	5	6	Not Used
Convenience of location	1	2	3	4	5	6	Not Used
Other _____	1	2	3	4	5	6	

ADMINISTRATION:

Joining instructions
— timeliness   1 2 3 4 5 6   Not Used
— adequacy   1 2 3 4 5 6   Not Used
Handling of any enquiries   1 2 3 4 5 6   Not Used
Other _____   1 2 3 4 5 6

7. GENERAL COMMENTS

Please add any comments which may help us improve the quality of the training experience, ie in terms of meeting your expectations and needs, making the programme more relevant to your job, providing a high quality of training and facilities.

Appendix 18.2   Reaction level questionnaire (simple)

DELEGATE ASSESSMENT OF THE TRAINING PROGRAMME

Course title: _____   Course date: _____

Name: _____   Manager's name: _____

Job title/grade: _____   Job title/grade: _____

Department: _____

We want to ensure that the training you receive is of high quality and of relevance to your job. We would be grateful if you would complete this questionnaire as frankly and as fully as possible.

---

1. BEFORE THE COURSE

Did you receive a pre-course briefing from your manager?
Yes ☐   No ☐

Did you receive joining instructions for the course?
Yes ☐   No ☐

If Yes, please indicate your views on the quality of the briefing and instructions by ticking the appropriate box:

	Poor quality	Fair quality	Good quality	Very good quality
Briefing prepared me well for the course (about what I was supposed to learn, why I was on the course, relevance to my job)	☐	☐	☐	☐
Instructions received in good time	☐	☐	☐	☐
Instructions were clear	☐	☐	☐	☐

2. ON THE TRAINING COURSE

Please indicate your views on the quality of the course by ticking the appropriate box:

	Poor quality	Fair quality	Good quality	Very good quality
Meeting the learning objectives	☐	☐	☐	☐
Relevance to your job	☐	☐	☐	☐
The trainer(s) helping you to learn	☐	☐	☐	☐
The handouts clear and useful	☐	☐	☐	☐
The adequacy of the training room(s)	☐	☐	☐	☐
The quality of the catering	☐	☐	☐	☐

3. GENERAL COMMENTS

Please add any comments which may help us improve the quality of your training.

Appendix 18.3 Reaction level questionnaire (trainer)

TRAINER FEEDBACK ON THE TRAINING COURSE

Course title: _____ Course date: _____

Name: _____ Organisation: _____
                              (if applicable)

Did you develop the course?   Yes ☐
                                No   ☐

How many times have you delivered this course?
Only this once ☐
2 – 5 times   ☐
6 + times   ☐

We want to ensure that the training delivered is as effective
as possible. We would be grateful if you would complete this
questionnaire.

---

1. TRAINING OBJECTIVES

Please comment on the extent to which you felt the training
objectives of the course were met and on any factors that
might have affected their achievement.

---

2. CONTENT, LEVEL AND LENGTH

Please comment on whether you felt the content, level and
length of the course were about right. If not, please put
forward some ideas for how the course can be improved.

---

3. TRAINING METHODS

Please comment on the effectiveness of the training methods used in meeting the training objectives.

4. FACILITIES AND ADMINISTRATION

a) Please comment on the adequacy and quality of the training facilities.

b) Please comment on the adequacy and quality of the general accommodation, catering and service.

c) Please comment on the quality of the administration both before and during the course.

5. GENERAL COMMENTS

Please add any comments which may help us improve the quality of the training experience, ie in terms of meeting the delegates' expectations and needs, making the programme more relevant to their jobs, providing a high quality of training and facilities.

Immediate Level
Evaluation

Introduction

Immediate level evaluation answers the question of the extent
to which delegates have *learned* from the training. It takes as
its starting point the training objectives for the course or
programme and the assessment is made against these objectives. It is critical that the training objectives:

● cover the span of the learning that is required
● are expressed in such a way that their achievement can be
  measured.

Chapter 12 described in detail how training objectives should
be formulated and proposed that a well-formed objective
should set out the performance that is required in behavioural terms, any conditions under which the performance will take place and criteria or standards of acceptable
performance. Successful immediate evaluation relies critically on the training objectives being well formed.
  There are two types of immediate level evaluation:

● the first measures whether the training objectives have
  been achieved, ie whether the delegates have reached the
  required standard or level of competence, and assessment
  takes place only at the end of the training.
● the second measures the gain in learning and therefore
  assessment is required both before and after the training.

What do the results tell us?

Immediate level evaluation takes place in the training
environment and gives feedback on the training delivery

process itself and on the training needs analysis. Poor results will indicate that the course has been ineffective in meeting the training objectives. There are basically two types of poor result:

- the results are poor for only a small number of delegates
- the results are generally poor for all delegates.

If the results are poor only for one or two delegates, this might suggest that the course was inappropriate for those particular delegates, ie there was a poor fit between training need and the training delivered for those delegates. Or, it could suggest that those delegates had not approached the training in a positive way, for whatever reason or in some way the relationship between the trainer and these delegates had not proved productive. Clearly, it is important to identify the cause of the problem so that appropriate action can be taken to remedy the situation for those delegates. The Training Professional also needs to keep an eye out for patterns − is it always delegates from an ethnic minority group or a particular department who achieve poor results? If such a pattern emerges, then a more major intervention might be required as it might suggest that the training is culturally biased, the trainer has difficulty relating to particular groups, or that training is not being supported/ encouraged in particular areas, etc.

However, from the Training Professional's point of view, the more critical situation arises when the results are generally poor. Identifying the causes requires some detective work. The possible causes could be with:

- the performance of the trainer(s)
- the training methods used
- the content/level of the course
- or any combination of these.

The first two are concerned with development and delivery part of the training cycle and the third would suggest that the training needs analysis was inadequate in that it had not correctly specified the training need. This is when the reaction level evaluation can be very useful as it is likely that the delegates themselves will have identified the problem area. The other obvious source of readily available information is the trainer — which is when trainer reaction level questionnaires come into their own. If the case is still unsolved, interviewing the trainer and a sample of the delegates may provide the answers.

How do we do it?

How we tackle immediate level evaluation usually depends on the nature of the learning that is taking place. Chapter 9 describes the three types of competencies and, hence, learning:

- knowledge
- skills
- attitudes.

We will look at each in turn.

Knowledge

Knowledge learning is most often assessed using some form of self-complete questionnaire. There are three basic types:

- a simple questionnaire that requires the delegate to answer either yes/no/don't know or true/false/don't know to a list of statements
- a multiple-choice questionnaire which may offer the delegate a number of choices of answer
- an open-ended questionnaire which requires free form essay-type answers.

The first two types of questionnaire are most useful for testing knowledge of rules and regulations and simple procedures. The third type of questionnaire is most useful for testing delegates' understanding of more complex subjects or how they may react to more complex situations. The first two types of questionnaire require very careful design, but then are quick and straightforward to assess. Care needs to be taken over how the questions are phrased and in the case of the multiple-choice questionnaire the range of choices and the positioning of the correct choice needs to be thought through. The open-ended questionnaire is usually easier to design, but then is more difficult to assess. It is important to draw up a clear and comprehensive marking scheme for this type of questionnaire. With all the questionnaires it is important that the questions are clear and unambiguous.

Examples of the three types of knowledge assessment questionnaires are shown as Appendices 19.1 to 19.3. They are all based on a training programme on how to handle disciplinary situations in a particular organisation. It can be seen that the first two deal with the fairly simple concepts of the knowledge of relevant employment law and organisational procedures. The third questionnaire is trying to assess delegates' knowledge and *understanding* of the procedures and how they would handle particular situations. However, obviously there is more to this than just simple knowledge; the delegates will need to develop some skills in handling the people involved in disciplinary situations − see the next section on skills assessment. Most courses involve both knowledge and skills learning and therefore a range of assessment methods may be required.

Assessing knowledge can be carried out for the two purposes:

- ensuring a required standard or level of competence has been reached − this will often be expressed in terms of achieving a minimum mark of, say, 80 per cent
- assessing gain in learning − which is often expressed in terms of a gain ratio (see Chapter 23).

The first approach is essential if a required standard must be reached before the delegate can take on a new job or some new duties, eg such as knowledge of safety procedures for driving a train or cash handling knowledge for staffing a checkout. Often in these cases establishing a learning gain is not relevant, as the starting knowledge is assumed to be zero or close to zero. The second approach − assessing gain in learning − is more useful where there is no absolute require-ment for a certain level of knowledge to be achieved before the delegate leaves the course and where delegates may come to the training programme with different starting levels of knowledge. It is most often used for management training and usually its primary purpose is the assessment of the course rather than the delegates, although the 'after training' results can also provide useful feedback on whether further help/support is required by individual delegates.

Skills

Skills-based learning is assessed by observation. Successful skill assessment is based on two key factors:

- the design of the assessment/observation process and form;
- the use of trained observers.

First, the skill needs to be broken down into its main ele-ments. For a relatively simple skill, eg changing a plug, there may be only four or five elements. For a more complex skill, eg wiring a fire alarm board, there may be considerably more. The assessment form will list all the different elements and each of these will be assessed. Since many technical skills require some form of qualification or licence, the methods and approaches for assessing technical skills are usually well established. The assessment may require the use of sophisti-cated simulation equipment, eg as exists for testing train-driving skills.

The assessment of management skills is generally less well developed, largely because it is rare to find a qualification of any sort being a prerequisite for the job in the same way as there often is for jobs using technical and professional skills. Also, the assessment of management skills is sometimes per-ceived as being difficult to do and often attempts are limited to knowledge assessments. However, the skill assessment is based on exactly the same principle of breaking down the skill into its key elements. The equivalent to the simulation

213

set-up is that some form of role playing is involved, eg assessing a mock appraisal interview or a mock presentation.

However, with skills such as interviewing, counselling and dealing with grievances the standards to be achieved and hence the assessment is less clear cut than with say a technical skill, where generally there is only one correct way and the standard of the finished 'product' can be very precisely defined. There is a much greater potential for subjectivity and hence the need for a well designed observation process and form, and for trained observers, becomes even more important. Also, because of the element of subjectivity and the complexity of what is being observed it is often helpful to have more than one observer.

Assessing skills is far more resource intensive than assessing knowledge, as the ratio of trainers/observers to delegates is at least one to one at the assessment stage. It can also extend the length of the course for the delegates. This is another reason why if there is not an absolute requirement for delegates to have reached a specific standard this type of assessment is often not done. The skills will be practised, using role plays, etc and observed with feedback given as part of the *development* of the skill, but not then *assessed* that a required level has been reached. Instead some training programmes build in an assessment in the workplace, ie an intermediate level assessment, for example, observing a trainer delivering a course for real, or a manager chairing an actual meeting – more about this form of assessment in the next chapter. However, as soon as you move outside the training environment other factors can start to intervene – how much opportunity for practice has there been, how much coaching/support has been received from the delegate's manager, how do you standardise the situation being assessed, eg the degree of difficulty or complexity of a meeting. The direct assessment of learning from the course is lost.

Appendix 19.4 provides an example of a simple assessment form for a management skill, selection interviewing, and Appendix 19.5 provides a more complex assessment form for assessing the skill of carrying out a disciplinary hearing. This latter form would comprise part of a package of assessment tools, together with the knowledge forms in Appendices 19.1 to 19.3, for assessing all aspects of a training programme for handling disciplinary situations. These forms can also be used for intermediate evaluation − assessment of performance back in the job where observing a *real* interview or disciplinary hearing would be the basis for the assessment.

As with the assessment of knowledge learning, skill assessment can be carried out for the two purposes of:

- ensuring that a required standard of competence is achieved, eg passing the driving test, gaining a certificate/licence in welding
- assessing gain in skills.

In practice, it is usually the first question that is addressed. This is often because either the skill is new and therefore the starting point is no skill, or because of the difficulties (cost/time) of assessment, establishing a starting point becomes impractical.

Attitudes

Assessing this third type of learning, attitudes, is particularly difficult. This is because often delegates are aware of the right answers to give. Also, many people might argue that it is very difficult to change attitudes and what you are aiming to change is the way people actually behave. This can both be a long process and one where the results are best measured where the behaviours will operate, ie in the workplace. This is discusssed further in the next chapter on intermediate level evaluation.

Some key issues

Developing immediate level evaluation tools usually requires specialist knowledge and will require liaison between the trainer and the specialist manager in the area. Developing these tools puts the training objectives under great scrutiny and can be a very useful way of ensuring that the training objectives do reflect the learning required from the course.

Equally, it is vital that the assessment tools do assess delegates on what the training objectives actually states the delegates will be able to do and neither more nor less. For example, if the training objective requires the delegate to be able to complete a specific form, eg an accident report form, then the assessment should involve the completion of that form based, say, on the description of an accident. In assessing whether this objective has been achieved, it would not be much use to ask the delegate only to state the sections that need to be filled in or, on the other hand, to require the delegate to write a management report on all the action needed to be taken as result of the accident!

It is important, also, to keep assessment tools up to date. For example, procedures change and standards can change. Sometimes, because immediate level assessment tools require considerable effort to develop they can get set in tablets of stone and continue to be used when they have ceased to be an appropriate method of assessment.

Another potential issue to be aware of is that of creeping reduction in standards through sloppy administration of assessments. For example, assessment questions can get to be well known and trainers can develop bad habits of giving heavy hints about what the questions are going to be. Marking standards can also drift if these are not monitored.

It is important, too, to bear in mind the two purposes of assessment tools:

- to licence individual delegates as competent in a particular knowledge area or skill
- to measure the effectiveness of the course in meeting the training objectives.

The first purpose can usually be addressed in a relatively straightforward way, eg by setting a standard that the delegate must achieve an 80 per cent result in a knowledge test or a particular rating in a skills test. The second purpose involves taking the results as a whole and perhaps looking at the proportion of delegates that passed the test, the average mark or score gained or where appropriate the average learning gain.

Finally, be aware that delegates can see assessment as frightening and worrying. It is important to make it very clear what the assessment is for. Is it to assess the delegate has reached a particular standard? If it is, then this should be explained at least at the outset of the course and preferably before the delegate is sent on the course. It should be made crystal clear how the assessment is going to be made, eg written tests, skill simulation, and the standard that is required. Also it is important that you and the delegate know what will happen if the delegate does not reach the required standard. Can the delegate resit the test and, if so, how many times over what period? If not, or if the delegate fails the resits, what happens then? If learning gain is being measured this is usually primarily to measure the effectiveness of the training — make this clear. Who will have access to the results, particularly individual results? Care needs to be taken when introducing assessment for the first time onto a course and, even more so, where it involves delegates who are not used to being assessed, for example, on management courses.

Conclusion

Immediate level evaluation is an important stage in the evaluation process. It directly measures the extent to which the training objectives have been achieved. Successful immediate level evaluation depends critically on the training objectives being well formed and a useful by-product of immediate evaluation is that it puts the spotlight on the training objectives. Designing the immediate level evaluation instruments during the TNA process can help ensure the appropriateness of the training objetives.

We now move on to the next evaluation level — measuring the effects of training on job performance.

Appendix 19.1 Handling disciplinary situations – Immediate level evaluation (knowledge/simple)

The purpose of the questionnaire is to get feedback on how successful the course has been. Individual results will be regarded as confidential. Please answer the following questions. Do not dwell too long over your answers but rely on your initial reaction. Fill in the box for the answer you have selected – T for a true statement, F for false and DK for don't know. Please do not guess; if you do not know the answer, fill in the box 'don't know'.

1. The sole purpose of discipline is punishment.

2. After hearing all the evidence you should always adjourn a disciplinary hearing to consider your decision.

3. Circumstances should always be taken into account when deciding on a case of discipline.

4. It can be fair for people to be given different punishments even though they have committed the same 'crime'.

5. The disciplinary process should be used to teach employees the 'rules'.

6. Under the disciplinary procedure an employee is entitled to have union representation when a witness statement is being taken down.

7. Gross misconduct is generally seen as misconduct serious enough to destroy the contract and make any further working relationship and trust impossible.

8. The rules of natural justice provide that a person subject to the disciplinary process may call witnesses in their defence.

9. The circumstances of the case against a shop steward should be discussed with a full-time official before any disciplinary action is taken.

10. An appeal should be made within five working days of receipt of notice of the punishment.

11. Breaches of disciplinary rules should be disregarded after a specified period of time.

12. An employee can appeal against an informal oral caution.

13. An employee may be dismissed for a 'first offence'.

14. A final written caution will warn that dismissal will result if there is no satisfactory improvement.

15. An employee has to have been employed by the Company for two years before s/he can bring a claim for race or sex discrimination.

16. A written warning will always set out the right of appeal.

17. An industrial tribunal will take into account the details of a case *and* the way it has been handled.

18. Except in cases of race or sex discrimination, an employee has to have been employed by the company for two years before s/he can bring a claim for unfair dismissal.

19. Shop stewards are subject to the same disciplinary standards as any other employee.

20. Sexual and racial harassment will always be considered by the company for disciplinary action.

Appendix 19.2   Handling disciplinary situations – Immediate level evaluation (knowledge/multiple choice)

The purpose of this questionnaire is to assess the effectiveness of the course. Individual results will be treated as confidential. Please tick the appropriate box. Please do not guess; if you don't know the answer tick the 'don't know' option.

1.	The main purpose of discipline is:	Punishment	☐
		Teaching a lesson	☐
		Improved performance	☐
		Don't know	☐
2.	When you have heard the evidence at a disciplinary hearing you should adjourn to consider your decision:	Always	☐
		Sometimes	☐
		Never	☐
		Don't know	☐
3.	When deciding on what punishment is appropriate for a breach of discipline, circumstances should be taken into account:	Always	☐
		Sometimes	☐
		Never	☐
		Don't know	☐
4.	It can be fair for people to be given different punishments even though they have committed the same 'crime':	Always	☐
		Sometimes	☐
		Never	☐
		Don't know	☐

5.	The witness statements for a disciplinary hearing are given to the accused person:	Never	☐
		At the disciplinary hearing	☐
		With the Form DP1	☐
		Don't know	☐
6.	An employee is entitled to have a union representative or workplace colleague present when a witness statement is being taken:	Always	☐
		At the manager's discretion	☐
		Never	☐
		Don't know	☐
7.	Gross misconduct is the term given to describe behaviour which is:	Very serious and requiring disciplinary action to be taken	☐
		Serious enough to make any further working relationship and trust impossible	☐
		Requiring a very heavy sentence	☐
		Don't know	☐
8.	Among other things, the rules of natural justice provide that a person subject to the disciplinary process:	Can remain silent if they wish	☐
		May call witnesses in their defence	☐
		Can choose who will take their disciplinary hearing	☐
		Don't know	☐

9.	Before disciplinary action is taken against a shop steward, the case against him/her should always be discussed with:	A workplace colleague, not in a position of authority over the accused	☐
		A senior personnel officer	☐
		A full-time union official	☐
		Don't know	☐

10.	An appeal against a disciplinary penalty should be made within:	Eleven working days of notification	☐
		Three working days of notification	☐
		Five working days of notification	☐
		Don't know	☐

11.	A first written caution should be disregarded if a similar offence has not been committed within:	It is never disregarded	☐
		One year	☐
		Two years	☐
		Don't know	☐

12.	An employee may not appeal against:	A written caution	☐
		A verbal caution	☐
		An oral caution	☐
		Don't know	☐

13.	An employee may be dismissed for a first offence:	When gross misconduct or negligence is proven	☐
		At the discretion of the manager	☐
		Never	☐
		Don't know	☐
14.	A final written caution will warn that:	Dismissal will take place the next time you are accused of negligence	☐
		Dismissal will ensue if s/he fails to meet the required standards	☐
		None of the above	☐
		Don't know	☐
15.	Except in cases of race or sex discrimination an employee bringing a claim for unfair dismissal must have been employed by the company for at least:	Six months	☐
		One year	☐
		Two years	☐
		Don't know	☐
16.	A written caution will always set out:	The time limit for it to be disregarded for further disciplinary action	☐
		The right of appeal	☐
		The penalty for offending again	☐
		Don't know	☐

17.	An industrial tribunal will always take into account the details of the case and:	Who is involved at the hearing	☐
		The race and sex of the person making the appeal	☐
		The way the case has been handled	☐
		Don't know	☐
18.	Before an employee can bring a claim for race or sex discrimination s/he has to have been employed by the company for at least:	One year	☐
		Two years	☐
		No time limit	☐
		Don't know	☐
19.	Shop stewards are subject to:	Softer disciplinary standards than any other employee	☐
		Harsher disciplinary standards than any other employee	☐
		The same disciplinary standards as any other employee	☐
		Don't know	☐
20.	Sexual and/or racial harassment will be considered by the company for disciplinary action:	Always	☐
		Sometimes	☐
		Never	☐
		Don't know	☐

225

Appendix 19.3 Handling disciplinary situations — Immediate level evaluation (knowledge/essay type)

The purpose of this questionnaire is to assess the effectiveness of the course. Individual results will be treated as confidential. Listed below are six questions about handling a disciplinary hearing. Please answer all the questions on the answer sheets provided.

Time allowed: 30 minutes

1. When should a defendant get copies of the witness statements and why at this time?

2. If you are chairing a disciplinary hearing and the defendant will not answer questions, what should you do?

3. If you are chairing a disciplinary hearing and a defendant walks out in the middle of the proceedings, what should you do?

4. If you are chairing a disciplinary hearing and the defendant or his/her representative become abusive, what are your options?

5. After having heard the evidence and deciding that the defendant is guilty of the offence, what factors should you take into account in deciding on the penalty?

6. What information should be included in the record of the disciplinary hearing?

Appendix 19.4 Assessment form for observation of a recruitment interview — Immediate and intermediate levels of evaluation (skill)

For use:
1. at the end of a selection/recruitment training programme
   for observing a role play
or
2. 3–6 months after a selection/recruitment training
   programme for observing an actual interview.

The observer(s) (ideally for the role play assessment there would be two observers) should be positioned so that they are unobtrusive, but have a clear view of both interviewer and interviewee.

The form is intended to assess current levels of skill and provide a structured means of giving feedback. As well as giving a 'grading', there is space for comments to record reasons for the 'grading' — examples of good practice and where there is room for improvement. All observers should read the notes 'How to give feedback' before carrying out the assessment observer role.

Grading — the interview technique was of:
1 poor quality
2 fair quality
3 good quality
4 very good quality

INTRODUCTORY STAGE		COMMENTS
Warm welcome — made the candidate feel at ease	1 2 3 4	
Clear, useful introduction of his/herself (name, title, role)	1 2 3 4	
Clear statement of the purpose and structure of the interview	1 2 3 4	
Positive statement about note taking	1 2 3 4	

ACQUIRING INFORMATION COMMENTS

Good use of open questions to open up topic areas	1 2 3 4
Good use of probing questions to follow up areas of interest	1 2 3 4
Avoidance of leading questions	1 2 3 4

GIVING INFORMATION COMMENTS

Clear and relevant details of the job	1 2 3 4
Clear and appropriate details of the company	1 2 3 4
Clear and appropriate details of conditions and pay	1 2 3 4

ENDING STAGE COMMENTS

Sufficient and supportive opportunities for questions from the interviewee	1 2 3 4
Clear indication of what will happen after the interview	1 2 3 4
Sincere and warm thank you	1 2 3 4

OVERALL COMMENTS

Good balance of time spent talking by interviewer (1 > 60%, 2 = 40–60%, 3 = 25–40%, 4 < 25%)	1 2 3 4
Good listening skills – indicated by following up leads, showing active listening	1 2 3 4
Good rapport (relationship) between interviewer/interviewee	1 2 3 4
No indications of sex or race bias	1 2 3 4

GENERAL COMMENTS

Appendix 19.5   Assessment form for observation of a disciplinary hearing − Immediate and intermediate levels of evaluation (skill)

For use:
1. at the end of a training programme on handling disciplinary situations for observing a role play
   or
2. 3 − 6 months after training programme on handling disciplinary situations for observing an actual disciplinary hearing.

The observer(s) (ideally for the role play assessment there would be two observers) should be positioned so that they are unobtrusive, but have a clear view of the proceedings.

The form is intended to assess current levels of skill and provide a structured means of giving feedback. As well as giving a 'grading', there is space for comments to record reasons for the 'grading' − examples of good practice and where there is room for improvement. All observers should read the notes 'How to give feedback' before carrying out the assessment observer role.

Grading − the technique was of: 1 poor quality
2 fair quality
3 good quality
4 very good quality

Conduct of disciplinary hearing

OPENING					COMMENTS
Clear introduction of him/herself	1	2	3	4	
Clear introduction of other panel members	1	2	3	4	
Details of defendant checked	1	2	3	4	
Clear statement that hearing part of disciplinary procedure	1	2	3	4	
Clear statement of charge	1	2	3	4	
Right to representation covered appropriately	1	2	3	4	

MAIN PART					COMMENTS
Good use of open questions to open up issues of concern	1	2	3	4	
Good use of probing questions to follow up issues of concern	1	2	3	4	
Avoidance of leading questions	1	2	3	4	
Good listening skills demonstrated	1	2	3	4	
Calm approach	1	2	3	4	
Effective control of hearing	1	2	3	4	
Impartiality displayed	1	2	3	4	
All evidence covered	1	2	3	4	
Adequate opportunity for defence provided	1	2	3	4	
Circumstances fully covered	1	2	3	4	

Was an adjournment held?   Yes ☐   No ☐   (please tick)

GIVING THE DECISION					COMMENTS
Clear statement of decision	1	2	3	4	
Clear statement of penalty taking account of previous discipline record	1	2	3	4	
Clear statement of penalty with any circumstances affecting it	1	2	3	4	
Clear statement of improvement sought (standard/target and timescale)	1	2	3	4	
Competent handling of any questions	1	2	3	4	
Full explanation of appeal process	1	2	3	4	

Quality of process

PREPARATION					COMMENTS
Notification to defendant timely and appropriate	1	2	3	4	
Location/layout/ arrangements appropriate	1	2	3	4	
Evidence assembled competently	1	2	3	4	

DECISION MAKING					COMMENTS
Appropriate decision made	1	2	3	4	
Circumstances properly taken into account	1	2	3	4	
Precedents taken into account	1	2	3	4	
Appropriate penalty given	1	2	3	4	
Appropriate documentation completed	1	2	3	4	

20

Intermediate Level
Evaluation

Introduction

Intermediate level evaluation measures the effect of the training on *job performance*. It takes the evaluation one step further on. Immediate level evaluation assesses the learning that has taken place on the training programme. Intermediate level evalution assesses whether this learning, be it knowledge, skills or attitudes, has been successfully transferred back into the workplace. It assesses whether job performance has improved and in particular whether the identified performance gap has been bridged. There is little point in developing skills, etc if they cannot be transferred back into the workplace. For most training programmes this is probably the most crucial level of evaluation. Therefore it is perhaps surprising that this level of evaluation is so infrequently carried out in any systematic way.

If the training needs analysis has been carried out properly, the performance gap will have been clearly identified and the indicators of required performance specified as precisely as possible. This makes intermediate evaluation a relatively straightforward activity. The problems come when these performance indicators have not been established at the outset and, to compound the difficulty, the level of pre-training performance has not been measured. However, do not despair, intermediate evaluation can still be tackled although it becomes harder and usually the results are less informative. The message again in this chapter is that designing the evaluation should be done at the same time as developing the training programme. Not only does it ensure that, where required, pre-training assessments may be carried out but also it again puts the spotlight on the adequacy of the training needs analysis and, very importantly, at a time when something can be done about it. If the questions of what performance is required at the end of the training and how will it be measured can *not* be answered then it begs the question of how can effective training be developed and designed?

What do the results tell us?

So, what happens if there are poor intermediate level evaluation results? Consider, again, these two situations:

- the results are poor only for a few delegates
- the results are generally poor.

If the results are poor only for a few delegates, the starting point is to look at the immediate level evaluation results for those delegates. If these were fine, then it would suggest there were specific factors in the workplace or personal to the individual that hampered the transfer of the learning back to the job. These could be that the individual's job had changed or the delegate had been away ill. Or of more concern, perhaps that the delegate was not receiving the required help and support from their manager. It could also simply be that the particular delegates should not have been sent on the training programme at all and the learning was not relevant to their jobs. These cases need to be investigated and again, as for the other levels of evaluation, it is important to be on the lookout for patterns and trends. Is it always particular departments, particular types of delegate, etc?

If the results are generally poor, again you should start with the immediate level results. If these were poor then the intermediate level results would not be surprising! However, it would beg the question of why no action was taken in response to the poor immediate level results. It highlights an extremely important point − it is vital to act on evaluation results. Only one thing is worse than ineffective training and that is knowing the training is ineffective and doing nothing about it! However, if the immediate level results were fine (and, of course, that the immediate level evaluation was appropriate) then it will have been established that the training objectives of the training programme have been achieved. If the learning represented by achievement of the training objectives has not resulted in the achievement of job performance objectives, it could suggest that the training had not tackled the right learning issues, ie that the training objectives were inappropriate, and therefore that the training needs analysis (TNA) on which they had been based was flawed. On the other hand, it is possible that there are some general factors/obstacles in the workplace that have hindered the transfer of learning back into the job. It may be that these could have been anticipated during the TNA process and addressed by the training or they may have occurred subsequently, perhaps a change of management leading to different priorities. The Training Professional must again don his/her deerstalker and magnifying glass and do some detective work!

If there are no immediate level results then the detective work becomes harder. You do not know whether it is the delivery of the training that is the problem, or the training that is inappropriate to the needs, or whether there are factors in the workplace that are affecting the results. The reaction level evaluation will prove a useful starting point again and then follow-up interviews with delegates and their managers can be helpful. Some organisations very successfully use group discussions involving delegates and their managers to investigate these issues.

How do we do it?

The basic choice with assessing the impact of training on job performance is between:

- assessing the behaviour in the workplace arising from the training
- measuring the results that delegates achieve (which is moving into the area covered by ultimate level evaluation).

Results versus behaviour assessment

There is a school of thought that argues *how* people do their jobs is not important, only the results achieved. Now for some sorts of training this may be the best approach, for example, the best indicator of sales training performance may well be the level of sales achieved or percentage of calls that result in business. Similarly, if the training is addressed at wordprocessing operators, then the appropriate measures may be speed of typing, ie words per minute, together with a quality measure such as number of errors per 1,000 words. However what happens if it is a course on customer care for staff working on the shop-floor of a department store. It may be possible to measure a performance indicator such as number of customer complaints − but even this may not be straightforward: are the complaints all down to customer service on the shop-floor or could the quality of the products be causing some of the problems? If only one or two members of staff have been trained, would you expect an impact on the number of complaints? Anyway, is looking at the level of complaints enough? Surely, you are hoping for good customer service not just a level of service that avoids complaints!

So, quite often the evaluation will need to look at how the job is done. So how do we do this? There is a range of approaches which involves decisions about:

- who does the assessment
- what method of assessment is used.

Who does the assessment?

There are usually three main choices of who does the assessment:

- the delegate, ie self-assessment
- the delegate's manager
- an external/independent assessor.

The most common approach is for self-assessment and

manager assessment and, quite often, a combination of the two. The advantages are that such assessments can usually form part of the normal working situation and therefore are low cost. They can also reinforce the coaching/mentoring role of the manager. The advantages of external assessors are that they are usually trained for the task, arguably make more objective assessments and can ensure consistency of standards.

For some sorts of training other assessors may come into play, for example:

- the delegate's subordinates − for training programmes, say, on leadership, appraisals, etc. Clearly, this can present sensitivity issues as in many organisations upward assessment is not well developed. In one organisation, this problem was addressed by using a regular anonymous employee satisfaction survey as the vehicle for the assessment. This was a credible approach as the training programme was being addressed at all managers in specific business units.
- the delegate's peers − for training programmes, say, on teamworking, time management, etc. Again, this sort of approach may need careful handling as peer assessment is similarly not well established in most organisations.

Methods of assessment

The methods of assessment are the familiar choice of:

- observation
- self-complete questionnaires
- interviews.

Observation

It is, perhaps, self-evident that the most direct way to assess *how* something is done is usually to observe it. What one would really like to do is be the proverbial fly on the wall. In practice, observing behaviour in the workplace has a number of problems. If it is specially set up for assessment purposes, ie *formal* observation, then it can be a time consuming and costly approach. It requires an observer/delegate ratio of at least one to one. If it is a particular skill, for example a technical skill such as welding a joint, then the observation can be very focused and of relatively short duration. Similarly, if it is a management skill such as giving a presentation, then the observation can be based on the specific occasion of giving a presentation. However, if it is a management skill such as handling poor performance situations which are not pre-planned, then it may require a considerable period of observation to witness the situations that give rise to the behaviour being assessed. Also where any formal observation is involved and in particular if formal observers (ie observers who would not normally form part of the workplace environment) are used, then the very presence of the observer can have an effect on the result (the Hawthorne effect, see p 83). If formal observation is used then the same types of assessment form as those used for the immediate evaluation of skills are appropriate (see Chapter 19). The only difference being that the delegate is performing the skill in the real environment of the workplace rather than under the simulated conditions of the training environment.

The introduction of National Vocational Qualifications (NVQs) and Scottish Vocational Qualifications (SVQs) has provided a competency structure and process for assessing many jobs. Many organisations are now designing their training programmes so that the measure of success of the effectiveness of the programme is the award of an NVQ/SVQ.

The alternative to the formal observation is the *informal* observation available through the normal manager-subordinate relationship. The manager will observe the delegate over a period of time performing the job areas addressed by the training and form a view of the level of competency achieved. This can then be used as a basis to ensure that the delegate has reached the appropriate standard and/or compared with a starting competency level to assess gain in competency.

Appendix 20.1 at the end of this chapter sets out one

approach to intermediate evaluation. It takes the delegate and the delegate's manager through the stages of:

- nomination onto the course, when the business need, and current and required levels of performance are identified
- a pre-course briefing between the delegate and his/her manager to ensure that the delegate is well prepared for the training
- a post-course briefing (usually within a couple of weeks of the training) between the delegate and his/her manager when:
  - the delegate's reaction to the course can be discussed (an alternative or additional approach to the self-complete reaction level questionnaire discussed in Chapter 18)
  - any further action required to support the training identified
- a post-course evaluation, after an appropriate time has elapsed, when post-course job performance is assessed and whether the business need has been met (moving into ultimate level evaluation).

With a new recruit or upon promotion or transfer into a new job, where the training is directed at providing the delegate with the full range of knowledge and skills required for the job, it is likely that the assessment will take place shortly after training and the full range of competencies for the job will need to be measured. Where the training is to improve or extend performance in an existing job, where practice and experience is part of the learning process, then it is likely that full assessment may not be appropriate for some months after the training (see Some Key Issues below). The assessment will probably only be against a partial set of competencies. The assessments can be based on either the formal or informal observation methods discussed earlier.

This approach to intermediate evaluation can have the additional and very important benefit of supporting the transference of the learning back into the job. It requires both the manager and the delegate to focus on the training process from start to finish, ie from identification of need and nomination through to assessment of whether the training has achieved the objectives in terms of job performance. It provides a structured means of ensuring that support is given at all stages and action taken when problems occur. It could be argued that the additional benefit of this approach is of equal and possibly even of greater value than the original evaluation process.

Where an appraisal system is in place, this approach can be linked in with it. This is particularly appropriate if it is an appraisal system based on more frequent meetings than the traditional annual appraisal, eg quarterly meetings.

Self-complete questionnaires

The alternatives to observation are interviews and self-complete questionnaires. Self-complete questionnaires have the advantage that they are a relatively low-cost method of collecting information. Again they can be directed at the delegates, their managers or both (or any other groups involved, eg peers). However, in order to extract the quite complex information that is required self-complete questionnaires need to be carefully designed to keep them as short and structured as possible. The types of question that are useful to ask are:

- How often has the skill/knowledge been used?
- How successful was the use of the skill/knowledge — either using a rating scale of some sort, or asking for examples of outcomes?
- How competent does the delegate and/or the delegate's manager rate the delegate both before and after the course?
- What barriers are there to, or problems with, using the skill/knowledge?

An example of a self-complete questionnaire designed to assess the effects of a time management course on job performance is given as Appendix 20.2.

Clearly there are advantages and disadvantages to relying only on self-assessment. It could well be argued that the delegate is the best source of information on his/her own behaviour. Hamblin (1974) argues that the problems associated with *objective* observation are such that:

> we shall regard the trainee himself as the main source of information.

On the other hand, there is the question of whether the delegate either will be willing to self-assess honestly or be able to self-assess accurately. On the first point a key question is anonymity. It is likely that the delegate will be more willing to assess his/her own performance honestly if there is no danger of the information being used for other purposes, eg the annual pay round! However, with this approach there is no opportunity to respond to the answers and take action where there are problems. To complete Hamblin's quote above:

> and we shall regard the evaluator as being primarily a catalyst whose aim is to achieve rapport with the trainee and so help the trainee to understand his own behaviour and plan how to change it.

Hamblin strongly took the view that the evaluation must be for the benefit of the delegate. In the case of self-complete questionnaires there is the possibility of conflict between the objective of the evaluation for assessing the effectiveness of the training, when anonymity may be advantageous, and meeting the needs of the delegate by providing further help and support if the training has been ineffective in some way, when clearly the delegate needs to be identified.

Interviews

The last method for consideration is that of interviews. There are the three potential approaches discussed earlier (Chapter 17):

- one-to-one, face-to-face interviews
- telephone interviews
- group interviews.

The first approach is quite a common method used although it falls between the two stools of low cost (self-complete questionnaires) and the most direct method (observation). Face-to-face interviews are costly, but with skilled interviewers a much greater degree of probing can take place than with a self-complete questionnaire. Also, the use of more sophisticated approaches, such as using repertory grid methods (see Chapter 10) can provide more rigorous and objective information. The compromise can be to build the evaluation into the normal appraisal system as suggested earlier or simply by adding onto the normal appraisal interview questions specifically aimed at the job performance which is the subject of the evaluation.

An alternative approach can be to use group interviews or discussion usually either with delegates or their managers. As well as a direct method of assessment this approach can be a particularly useful way of identifying problem areas. For example, if the evaluation using assessment questionnaire surveys or manager assessment is coming up with poor results, then group discussion can be a very effective way of distilling out the causes.

Some key issues

Perhaps the most important issue is to take into account that this level of evaluation involves assessment *in the workplace.* It will be vital to:

- secure the co-operation of all concerned and this means communicating clearly and in good time the purpose and benefits of the evaluation. It can mean sharing at the outset who is going to get the results and how they will be used
- ensure wherever possible it is of benefit to the individual delegates, so that it reinforces the training message and deals with unmet needs
- minimise the impact on the workplace − this usually means in terms of the time of those involved, usually the delegate and his/her manager.

Another important issue is that of timing — *when* the assessment should take place. This will depend on:

- whether the training is to carry out a new job or take on new skills, in which case the assessment is likely to be relatively soon after the training
- whether the training requires a period of practising the skills in the workplace, in which case it will depend on the period of time required. For example, if the skills are used on an everyday basis such as receptionist skills, computing skills, etc then the period of time may be quite short — perhaps a month or two. However, if the skill is practised less frequently, eg selection interviewing by a line manager, presentation skills, dealing with an emergency situation, or requires a longer period to develop the skills, eg leadership or time management skills, then a considerably longer period of time may need to elapse — three months or more
- if the evaluation requires observation and if informal observation is being used, eg by the delegate's manager, then there needs to be sufficient opportunity for observation to take place.

Ideally, with intermediate evaluation which involves the improvement of existing skills it is important to have an assessment of the skills before the training begins. If that option is not available, then an alternative approach is to establish the starting point, ie the before training level, at the time of the post training assessment. This clearly has the disadvantage that it may be hard to focus on behaviours of the past. However, it does have the advantage, and arguably this is a significant advantage when self-assessment is involved, that delegates at the later stage (ie after the training) will have a much clearer picture of the behaviours and standards of behaviours being assessed than before the training. In terms of the training model analogy — that people progress from unconscious incompetence through conscious incompetence to conscious competence and finally unconscious competence — it could be argued that before the training started people were in a state of unconscious incompetence as to the quality of their skills!

Conclusion

Intermediate level evaluation is potentially the most valuable source of information for assessing the effectiveness of training. However, it is also the level of assessment that requires the most careful and thoughtful planning and implementation to ensure that the information gathered is relevant and of good quality and at the same time causes least disruption in the workplace. Clear objectives, consultation with all the key players and careful testing of the assessment instruments used are all the essential ingredients of a successful evaluation study. We will continue this theme in the next chapter on ultimate level evaluation.

Appendix 20.1 Training nomination and evaluation package

Purpose

Training is designed to achieve improved workplace performance. To ensure that the training is as effective as possible requires a partnership between:

- the delegate − in preparing for the training, actively and conscientiously participating in the training and then applying the learning back into the job
- his/her manager − in providing support before and after the training
- the training manager − in ensuring the right course is chosen and evaluating the effectiveness of the training course
- the training deliverer − in ensuring that the quality of the training delivery is as high as possible.

The first stage is to identify clearly the business need and the gap between current standards and the required standards of performance. It is important to consider non-training solutions and informal training approaches before opting for a formal training course. The training need must then be closely matched to an appropriate training course.

This package is designed to ensure that the training delivered is as effective as possible. It involves a number of stages − the nomination of the delegate for the course, the preparation of the delegate for the training course, the professional delivery of the training and then the support and monitoring of the delegate after the course to maximise and measure the transference of the learning from the course to the job.

Stages in package

1. The nomination of the delegate for the course. This should be a joint approach to ensure that:

- the business need is clearly identified
- the current and required levels of performance are assessed
- all other approaches to bridging the gap are investigated
- a method and timescale for assessing performance after training is established
- any other details, eg any preferences for timing, deliverer, training methods and any special needs are specified.

245

2. Pre-course briefing for the delegate from the manager to ensure that:

- the training objectives of the course are understood
- the delegate clearly understands why s/he is on the course
- the delegate understands how the course relates to his/her job
- any pre-course preparation work required is identified
- any problems are identified which may affect the delegate's ability to make the most effective use of the training.

3. Training delivery.

4. Post-course training briefing and appraisal meetings:

- immediately following the training, a meeting between the manager and delegate to:
  a) discuss the delegate's reaction to the course
  b) identify any particular training needs not met and any action that is required to aid the transference of the learning to the job
- three months after the training or any period considered appropriate to assess the effect of the course on job performance and in meeting the business need
- at later stages if required.

DETAILS FORM A

Delegate name: _____   Manager's name: _____

Job title/grade: _____   Job title/grade: _____

Department: _____   Training manager: _____

NOMINATION FORM B

Describe business need.

Describe current level and required level of performance.

Why have you chosen a training solution?
(If appropriate, include what other solutions have been considered.)

What support will be given to ensure that the benefits of the training will be transferred to the job?

Explain how and when the effectiveness of the training will be measured.

Details of training required:

Date training is required by:

Any dates when individual is not available:

Any comments on type of training:

DETAILS OF TRAINING FORM C

Title: _____ Ref no (if applicable): _____

Delivery dates: _____

Trainer(s): _____

Training objectives. 1.

2.

3.

4.

5.

6.

PRE-COURSE BRIEFING FORM D

The pre-course briefing should take place ideally one to two weeks before the training course. The purpose is to ensure that the delegate is as well prepared as possible for the training course.

The areas to be covered are:

1. the competencies in the job that the training course is addressing
2. the training objectives of the course
3. any preparation work required before the course
4. any problems or concerns that the delegate might have that might affect his/her ability to make the best use of the course.

Date of briefing:

Comments:

Signed: Signed:

Manager   Delegate

POST-COURSE BRIEFING FORM E – COMPLETED IMMEDIATELY AFTER TRAINING COURSE

This form should be completed within two weeks of the delegate returning from the training course. Its purpose is to gauge the delegate's overall reaction to the course and identify any immediate area of unmet needs and any further action that may be required at this stage.

Details of how the full competency appraisal is to be carried out should also be discussed.

Date of briefing:

How does the delegate rate the course overall in preparing him/her for carrying out the job, please tick:

poor quality	☐
fair quality	☐
good quality	☐
very good quality	☐

Comment on why the course was fair or poor quality.

Are there any areas where further action is required at this stage (please tick): Yes ☐
No ☐

If Yes, please complete the box below.

AREAS WHERE FURTHER ACTION IS REQUIRED

This could take the form of manager support/coaching, self-learning, further training, a work/project assignment, any other appropriate activity.

AREA   PROPOSAL FOR ACTION   REVIEW DATE

Signed: Signed:

Manager   Delegate

EVALUATION FORM F

This form is to be completed three months (or whatever period is considered appropriate) after the training. The purpose is to assess how effectively the training has met the training needs and business needs identified in the Nomination Form B.

Date of evaluation form completion:

Describe current level of job performance in areas addressed by training. Is job performance up to the required standard? Please indicate how performance has been assessed.

Described if and how business need has been met.

If job performance is not up to required standard and/or business need has not been met, identify the reasons for this.

Proposals for further action if required.

Signed: Signed:

Manager   Delegate

251

Appendix 20.2 Intermediate level questionnaire for time management training course

The purpose of this survey is to evaluate how effective the time management training programme that you attended has been in improving your performance in your job. It is emphasised that it is not intended to assess your performance and all individual information collected will be treated confidentially. It is important that you answer the questions as honestly and fully as possible.

1. To what extent has the course helped in you prioritising and planning your workload? Please circle the appropriate rating.

   Not at all   1   2   3   4   5   6   Very much

2. Please tick if you were using any of the following techniques:

	Before the course	Now
Time log	☐	☐
A diary planner	☐	☐
Sorting in-tray	☐	☐
Other planning tools, please specify:		
_____	☐	☐
_____	☐	☐

3. To what extent has the course helped you control interruptions more effectively? Please circle the appropriate rating.

   Not at all   1   2   3   4   5   6   Very much

4. Please tick if you were using any of the following techniques:

	Before the course	Now	N/A
Keeping an interruptions log	☐	☐	
Secretary screening calls/visitors	☐	☐	☐
Colleague screening calls/visitors	☐	☐	☐
Use of surgery times	☐	☐	
Working in quiet place	☐	☐	
Booking meetings with yourself	☐	☐	
Others, please specify:			
_____	☐	☐	
_____	☐	☐	

5. How many meetings have you chaired since the course? Please tick the appropriate box.

No meetings ☐
1 – 3 meetings ☐
4 – 6 meetings ☐
7 or more meetings ☐

If your answer was *no meetings*, please go to Q8.

6. To what extent has the course helped you to chair meetings more effectively? Please circle the appropriate rating.

Not at all 1 2 3 4 5 6 Very much

7. Please tick if you have used any of the following techniques:

	Before the course	Now
Having clear meeting objectives	☐	☐
Using an agenda	☐	☐
Sending an agenda out in advance	☐	☐
Allocating times to agenda items	☐	☐
Specifying type of outcome for items, eg for information/ decision	☐	☐
Others, please specify:	☐	☐
	☐	☐

8. How many meetings have you participated in since the course? Please tick the appropriate box.

No meetings ☐
1 – 3 meetings ☐
4 – 6 meetings ☐
7 or more meetings ☐

If your answer was *no meetings*, please go to Q11.

9. To what extent has the course helped in you to participate in meetings more effectively? Please circle the appropriate rating.

Not at all 1 2 3 4 5 6 Very much

253

10. Please tick if you were using any of the following techniques:

	Before the course	Now
Requesting an agenda	☐	☐
Setting aside time to prepare for meeting	☐	☐
Attending for specific items only	☐	☐
Sending writing contributions when only involved in minority of items	☐	☐
Others, please specify:	☐ ☐	☐ ☐

11. To what extent has the course helped in you to delegate more effectively? Please circle the appropriate rating.

N/A   Not at all 1 2 3 4 5 6 Very much

If your answer is *N/A*, please go to Q13.

12. Please tick if you were using any of the following delegation techniques:

	Before the course	Now
Preparing written brief	☐	☐
Clarifying use of resources	☐	☐
Setting clear timescales	☐	☐
Setting up review meetings	☐	☐

13. Overall, how would you rate your time management skills before the course and now. Please circle the appropriate rating (1 indicating poor time management skills . . . 6 indicating very good time management skills).

Before the course 1 2 3 4 5 6

Now   1 2 3 4 5 6

14. Are there any problems or barriers to you implementing the time management skills that you learned on the training course?

15. Looking back on the course are there any comments or changes you would like to suggest for improving the effectiveness of the course?

In order to help us analyse the results of the survey it would be helpful if you could let us have some information about yourself:

Age   Sex   Ethnic Origin   Grade

≤ 25 years ☐ Male ☐ .... ☐ .... ☐
26−35 years ☐ Female ☐ .... ☐ .... ☐
36−45 years ☐ .... ☐ .... ☐
46−55 years ☐
56+ years ☐

21

Ultimate Level Evaluation

Introduction

Ultimate level evaluation is concerned with measuring the effects of the training on *organisational performance*. In terms of what we mean by organisational performance, this can range from an individual's performance, eg increased productivity, increased sales generated by a specific sales-person, through to performance indicators measured at the more global level such as turnover, profit, quality measures, eg customer satisfaction indices, error rates, absence rates. In the last chapter, we distinguished between the two ways of assessing job performance − assessing job behaviour or results. Intermediate evaluation is primarily concerned with looking at how people do their jobs, ultimate evaluation looks at the results of the changed performance and their impact on organisational performance.

You might argue that this is the key level of evaluation − surely the primary and *ultimate* purpose of training is to improve organisational performance. People can change the way they do their jobs until the cows come home but if this does not impact on the organisational performance then surely the training has failed? The answer to this question must be yes. Particularly, as we take as the starting point for this book that training must be directed to business needs. The starting point of any training needs analysis is what is the business need and the closing point of any evaluation must be whether the need has been met. Or maybe not quite the closing point since a further question may be whether the need has been met at an acceptable cost or in the most cost-effective way. These last questions will be tackled in the next chapter − in this chapter we will concentrate on looking at how you assess whether that ultimate business need has been met.

There are some situations where ultimate level evaluation may not be appropriate, however. For example, if the training is for someone to take on a new job, the business need is to have a trained employee in place at a certain time such as a train driver or checkout operator. Then, the measure of success is that the employee is assessed as competent in their job after the training. This lends itself more directly to intermediate level evaluation, although such assessment could involve measuring throughput and lack of errors on the checkout, etc.

The reason that ultimate level evaluation is often not tackled, when it is appropriate to do so, is because:

- There are no clear/obvious/direct performance measures, eg leadership training, time management, etc.
- Many factors other than training can intervene and affect results. For example, sales can be affected by general economic conditions or competitor initiatives, output can be affected by changes in machinery, staff retention rates by labour market conditions, customer satisfaction by factors other than the performance of retail staff. Perhaps there is more than one training programme taking place that may be contributing to change in performance.
- Performance measures often relate to whole units, eg departments or even the organisation as an entity. If the training is not directed at all the staff in the unit then it is very difficult to identify the effects of the training for the individual or group of staff that have been trained. For example, if only some of the staff in a department of a retail store have been trained in customer care, it would be difficult to assess the expected or achieved impact on customer complaints or level of sales.

These are all reasons that make ultimate level evaluation difficult and not a precise art. So, don't go for perfection or the ultimate in ultimate level evaluation − take a pragmatic view about what can be assessed. Be honest about what you are doing and what you are not doing − make clear any limitations or caveats with your evaluation results. This is just one more piece in the jigsaw.

How do we do it?

This can best be viewed as a five-stage process:

1 Identify the key indicator(s)/measure(s) of organisational performance that will be used for the assessment. These should be identified at the training needs analysis stage and fall directly out of the statement of business need giving rise to the training. Examples of the sorts of performance indicators that could be used are shown in Table 6.1.
2 Ensure results are available in the right form for the before training period.
3 Decide how long the training will take to affect the indicator. This encompasses the need for practice and skill development and also how long it will take before the changed performance will show up in the particular indicator. For example, improved selling skills may take several months to impact on orders taken and finally sales generated. This decision will also depend on how regularly the performance indicator is measured. For example, customer satisfaction surveys may only be undertaken every six months.
4 Identify the other factors that might intervene and consider methods for minimising or measuring the effects of the other factors. For example, by comparing results with other parts of the business where training has not taken place, ie using a form of control group. If the measure was sales performance, then both groups (the trained group and non-trained group) would have experienced the same economic and competitive conditions. (Clearly, it is important to ensure that this is the case, ie the control group is similar to the trained group in all relevant aspects − see Chapter 17.)
5 Set up appropriate systems to monitor the results. This is particularly important if the results are not usually monitored either at all or in the form required for evaluation purposes and also when the results are being monitored over a long period.

Table 6.1

Examples of measures/indicators of organisational performance

Type of training	Results that could be measured
Customer care training	Number of customer complaints (analysed by type of complaint) Customer satisfaction using surveys Number of customers Level of orders or sales Number of referrals from existing customers Number of lost customers Amount of repeat business
Supervisory or management training to deal with performance issues	Productivity measures Levels or output/sales Wastage rates Error rates Absenteeism Customer satisfaction Number of disciplinaries
Selection interview training	Percentage of offers accepted Percentage recruits deemed fully competent at the end of probation period Average length of time recruits stay
Safety training	Number of accidents (analysed by type and degree of seriousness) Results of safety audits Lost time due to injuries

Based on Robinson and Robinson (1989, p 263) and Boydell (1990, p 11).

Conclusion

In concept, perhaps ultimate evaluation is the easiest level of evaluation to understand. It answers the question of whether the original business need has been met. When there are clear indicators or measures of organisational performance which are directly affected by the training then the assessment process is straightforward and, on the face of it, objective. However, this is the ideal situation and, sadly, it is a rare Training Professional that experiences this. In practice, the choice of indicators is usually subjective and the extent to which the training is deemed to contribute to any changes in these indicators is also subjective.

The analogy of the jigsaw is apt. The different evaluation levels all provide different windows into the process or provide different pieces of this jigsaw labelled 'how effective is the training?' We move now to the last piece of this jigsaw. We have concentrated so far on assessing the results of the benefits from the training. The next chapter addresses the question of whether those benefits have been achieved at an acceptable cost.

22

Cost Effectiveness and Cost/benefit of Training

Introduction

The evaluation processes discussed so far have been aimed at looking at how well the training has met key objectives:

- delegates' satisfaction objectives – reaction level evaluation
- training objectives of the course – immediate level evaluation
- job performance objectives – intermediate level evaluation
- organisational objectives – ultimate level evaluation.

However, the other vital element in the equation is the cost of the training. It is a rare organisation where cost is of no concern! Therefore, there are two other important questions that need to be considered:

- Has the training been delivered in the most cost-effective way, ie at the least cost for achieving the objectives?
- Do the benefits of the training outweigh the costs or, expressed a little differently, does the training provide an adequate return on the investment made in it?

To a large extent the first of these questions will or should have been addressed through the process of systematic training needs analysis outlined in the earlier sections of this book. This process ensures that the training need is specified very precisely, ie the objectives are clear and measurable, and then examines how the training need can best be met, in terms of formal or informal training approaches, training methods used and make or buy decisions. However, cost effectiveness can also be assessed directly. For example, designing two different training programmes to meet the same training objectives — perhaps, using a distance learning approach and a traditional classroom approach. Both programmes would be assessed in terms of meeting the training objectives and business need, and evaluated against the costs.

The second question is perhaps the most fundamental as well as the most difficult question to address in the whole of the evaluation arena. Training is often described as an investment — usually because the term investment is perceived as a more positive term than describing it as a cost! However, because it is an investment in just the same way as building a new factory, buying a new item of equipment, buying stocks and shares, it requires an expenditure of money and resources by the organisation from which a return will be expected. Most major investments by organisations have to be justified in advance of the agreement to proceed. This is often done using some form of investment appraisal process which involves:

- assessing the expenditure required and the timing of the expenditure
- estimating the benefits that will result from the expenditure in monetary terms and when these benefits will accrue
- taking into account the time value of money, ie that the benefits are worth more the sooner they are achieved (discounting the value).

The appraisal will usually result in one of two measures:

- an *internal rate of return* for the project, eg 10 per cent, which is similar in concept to the interest rate that would be received if the money had been invested in a bank or building society
- a *net present value* for the project, expressed as a sum of money which represents the present value (value in today's terms) of a future flow of benefits over and above the original investment.

(Do not worry about calculating these measures, as it is easily done using a spreadsheet package such as Excel.)

The first method is perhaps most commonly used for large investment projects. Organisations will usually have a target rate of return that is required for projects to receive approval and after that, if there are limited funds, generally the projects with the highest rates of return will be chosen. However, there is yet another factor that needs to be taken into account − that of risk. With some projects the returns or benefits will be much less certain and organisations may often have to weigh up higher returns against higher risks.

Training projects often escape the rigorous financial discipline of this form of investment appraisal or indeed any financial assessment. The downside of this more financially relaxed approach has been that in times of cutback training often appears a soft option. It can be difficult to show any tangible financial rewards from training, whereas usually the production manager can *prove* what the effects would be of closing down a production line, or what would be the rewards from investment in new equipment and the distribution director can *prove* what the effects would be of cutting back the warehouse staff or the rewards would be from a new computerised stock control system.

So, assessing the costs and benefits or working out the rate of return from training would seem to have considerable merits. So, why is it not done more frequently? The assessments of the costs side of the equation is tedious but generally not hard. Chapter 13 sets out some of the costs of developing and delivering courses. Chapter 16 discusses approaches to accounting for the total costs of a course including the less tangible area of overheads. Newby (1992) goes into considerable detail on the assessment of costs and provides a useful guide to what should be included. Your finance specialists, too, should be able to advise on how to put together the costs of a training project. However, the other side of the equation, quantifying the benefits or returns from the training into monetary terms, can be very difficult.

Assessing benefits from performance indicators

Sometimes it can be straightforward to quantify the benefits. For example, if the training can be shown to produce a quantifiable:

- increase in sales
- increase in productivity/output
- reduction in wastage and hence in production costs
- reduction in accidents, equipment downtime, etc and hence in costs
- reduction in absence rates, labour turnover and hence in labour costs.

To demonstrate the principles, let's take a relatively simple example. Suppose a training programme has been devised for sales representatives aimed at increasing sales. The aim of the training programme is to increase sales by 10 per cent. Half the sales representatives are chosen at random to go on the training programme. The cost of the training is estimated at £200,000. It is estimated that the benefits of the training will last three years.

Sales for representatives on the course average £800,000 per month (measured over the last six months). The profit ratio for the firm is 8 per cent, ie the profit from every £100 of sales is £8.

End of year	Cash flow	
0*	− £200,000	
1	+ £76,800	Monthly increase in sales = 10% of £800,000 = £80,000;
2	+ £76,800	monthly increase in profits = 8% of £80,000 = £6,400;
3	+ £76,800	annual increase in profits = 12 × £6,400 = £76,800

(*The convention is to show expenditure as occurring at the end of year 0, ie the beginning of year 1 and benefits accruing at the end of the periods in which they occur.)

264

The internal rate of return (see pages 262–3) of this project is calculated as 7 per cent.

Assume the training project was accepted based on this appraisal. The results of the training would then be monitored using the sales results for the trained representatives. The untrained representatives would act as a control group. The performance measure would be:

annual sales of the trained group *minus* annual sales of the control group

As long as the additional sales were £76,800 or more each year then the original appraisal will have been justified. The use of the control group is to take into account other factors such as the economic and competitive situation and any natural trend in sales performance. If a control group had not been used then it would be important to take into account these other factors some other way, for example, perhaps by adjusting by the industry-wide increases in sales or simply estimating what the expected sales might have been without the benefit of training.

A seemingly simple appraisal of a training project turns out not to be so straightforward! In this example, the benefits from the training were readily quantifiable in concept at least. Sales are already expressed in a monetary form and the benefit to the organisation readily calculated through the profit ratio. The problems occurred when trying to identify what increase in sales could be attributed directly to the training.

British Telecom (Coaley, 1993) carried out a very interesting study to determine the 'financial' worth of some of their management training. They set out first to identify 'failure costs' due to poor performance by junior managers in the business. This was achieved by carrying out critical incident interviews (see Chapter 10) with the line managers. Performance ratings of the junior managers were made before and after the training. Achievement of a certain rating post training indicated that performance was 'normal, effective, acceptable' and therefore the failure costs due to poor performance would no longer occur. It was reported in

Personnel Management Plus (January, 1994) that BT's £7m investment in training was estimated to have brought a £280m return to the company (the net present value or worth to the company today of a flow of benefits over six years). Most finance directors would consider this an excellent return from their investment!

Assessing benefits using a value added approach

So, on now to the more tricky assessment of, for example, a general management course. In theory it may be possible to identify and measure performance indicators such as productivity increases, reduction in wastage, failure costs as British Telecom did, etc. However, in practice this can be very difficult and it is worth considering the alternative approach based on the concept developed by Cascio and Ramos (Cascio, 1991) that salary is the starting point for putting a value on performance:

> Assuming an organisation's compensation program reflects current market rates for jobs, then the economic value of each employee's labour is reflected best in his or her annual wage or salary.

This is the fundamental concept. There are the further issues of whether labour on-costs such as pension, National Insurance, cost of accommodation, etc or an individual's contribution to profit should also be included.

The approach at its simplest is based on assessing the performance of the delegate before the training, either on the whole job, or the part that is being addressed by the training and then again after training. Taking a very simple example, suppose that a delegate whose salary is £16,000 pa is being trained in leadership skills at a cost of £2,000. A job analysis identifies that the competencies being trained form 25 per cent of the full job. The delegate is assessed as being 60 per cent competent in this area before the training. The training is intended to bring the delegate up to full competence, ie 100 per cent.

Let us assume that the benefits of the training are £1,600

Added value from the training/year	= value of salary paid for leadership competencies × gain in competence
	$= £ (0.25 \times 16,000) \times \dfrac{(100-60)}{100}$
	$= £4,000 \times 0.4$
	$= £1,600$

for the first year, but that it is estimated that without the training the delegate would have increased in competence to 80 per cent through experience and coaching on the job after one year. The benefit for the second year would then be £800. After two years it is assumed that the delegate would have reached full competency without the training.

The appraisal would be based on:

End of year	Cash flow
0	− £2,000
1	+ £1,600
2	+ £800

The internal rate of return (see pages 262−3) on this training project is calculated as 15 per cent.

This looks nice and easy. Well, yes in a way it is − the concept is a very simple one. The hard part is the bit that is skipped over − assessing the competence level before and after the training and also taking a view about the way the benefits fall away over the period of time. Clearly this is a subjective assessment − probably by the delegate's manager. There are various approaches to analysing the job and assessing competence level or performance level including the use of performance grids and what is referred to as DIF (Difficulty, Importance, Frequency) analysis. Cascio (1991), although rather complex, and Jackson (1989, Chapters 4 and 5) provide useful further reading on these approaches.

Conclusion

Carrying out some form of cost/benefit analysis or investment appraisal requires thought and effort. For major training proposals, this should be an essential activity and there are considerable benefits from using the discipline of this approach for most reasonably sized training projects. It is very difficult if not impossible to carry out the perfect appraisal. What is required is a reasonable best attempt! All cost/benefit analyses and investment appraisals are littered with assumptions of one sort or another. So take heart and give it a try. The more you do them and experiment with different approaches the better you will become. As ever, always be clear and open about what has been done and what assumptions have been made. At least you will now be able to proffer some evidence to support the *belief* that training is worthwhile!

23

Analysing Evaluation Results

Introduction

Evaluation studies can generate a large quantity of what can be called *raw data*, the basic numbers that cascade out of our questionnaires, interviews, monitoring of performance indicators, etc. However, these numbers as they stand do not tell us very much. In an earlier book (Bee & Bee, 1990) we stated:

> Data on its own is meaningless, it must be converted into information before it can be used in the decision making process.

This chapter is going to look briefly at some of the most useful techniques for converting data into useful information. The purpose is to introduce you to the techniques and how they can be used. It is not the intention to bury you in statistical theory and formulae but, if you want to find out more about a technique, to refer you on to a couple of books in the field.

The advent of simple but sophisticated computer software has opened up the field of statistics to a much wider audience. Standard spreadsheet packages such as Excel and Lotus enable complex statistical functions to be calculated at the press of the button and statistical charts and diagrams to be produced in seconds. This is both good news and bad news for the Training Professional embarking on their analysis of evaluation results. The good news is that they can undertake quite sophisticated statistical analysis quite easily. The bad news is that they can be tempted down a sophisticated statistical path without really understanding what they are doing and therefore what the information produced really tells them and perhaps more importantly what it does not tell them. There are two basic messages to come out of this homily:

- keep your analysis as simple as possible
- if you do use a more sophisticated technique, make sure you understand it either by undertaking further reading or seeking help from a friendly statistician.

The starting point for any evaluation study must be the purpose or objective(s) of that study. This will guide the methodology and approach to the data collection. The analysis, too, should be undertaken with the objectives clearly in mind.

Purpose of analysis

There are generally four main purposes for analysing evaluation results:

- to summarise data – often a great mass of data is produced and it is necessary to reduce it down to a manageable form
- to compare data – results from different courses, between the trained group and the control group, etc
- to examine relationships between data – between results from immediate level evaluation and intermediate level evaluation, between the effectiveness of the training and size of training group, etc
- to highlight specific/problem areas – with meeting a particular training objective, with a particular trainer, etc.

This chapter is divided into two approaches – diagrammatic and numerical. Diagrammatic approaches use diagrams or pictorial representation to describe or present the information. Numerical methods rely on describing or presenting the information using a number or set of numbers. Both approaches are all about conveying the message – the message being sent by the evaluation results – in as clear and understandable a way as possible. The next two parts cover each in turn.

Diagrammatic approaches

Presenting data in a diagrammatic form can be a very powerful way of increasing the understanding and impact of that data. The most useful diagrammatic methods are:

- bar charts
- pictograms
- histograms
- pie charts
- graphs
- scatter diagrams.

Bar charts

A bar chart as the name suggests presents information in the form of bars – these can be vertical or horizontal bars. Each bar represents an item of information and the height/length of the bar represents the quantity of that item. This is a simple but very useful way for presenting information, particularly reaction level results – see Figure 6.3.

Pictograms

A pictogram is a form of bar chart where the bars are replaced by pictures representing the item of information. This can be a very eyecatching way of presenting the information and is particularly useful in making presentations and for reports that are aimed at audiences who are less familiar with statistical charts, eg if the evaluation results were being reported back to a group of non-management delegates – see Figure 6.4.

Histograms

A histogram is a special form of bar chart that is used to present frequency information. It is hard to describe, so look at Figure 6.5. This shows the ratings (marks out of 100 given to a training course) over a specific year. It shows the

the percentage of occasions that the course received ratings of, eg 51–60 per cent, 61–70 per cent. The main difference between bar charts and histograms is that, with the former, there is no relationship between the bars, ie they can appear in any order, whereas in the histogram there is. For ease of analysis and presentation make sure that your groups are the same size, eg in Figure 6.5 the data has been divided into 10 per cent ranges.

Pie charts

A pie chart or pie diagram is a powerful way to compare sections of the data relative to the whole. As the name suggests it presents the information in the shape of a pie or a circle. Each segment of the pie represents a part of the data. Figure 6.6 shows how delegates rated a trainer, split between four categories of ratings – very good, good, fair and poor. A segment can be highlighted by showing it as a cut slice of the pie, slightly withdrawn from the whole.

Graphs

Line graphs can be used to show trends in data over time – see Figure 6.7 showing training expenditure per employee over a six-year period – and also to show relationships between sets of data – see the paragraphs on correlation and regression below.

Scatter diagrams

Scatter diagrams are used to show relationships between sets of data – see Figure 6.8 and paragraphs on correlation and regression below.

Figure 6.3 *Simple bar chart*

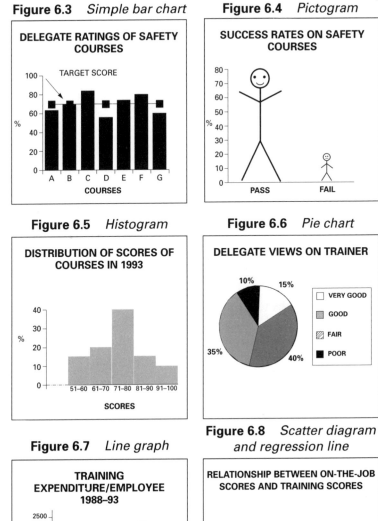

DELEGATE RATINGS OF SAFETY COURSES

Figure 6.4 *Pictogram*

SUCCESS RATES ON SAFETY COURSES

Figure 6.5 *Histogram*

DISTRIBUTION OF SCORES OF COURSES IN 1993

Figure 6.6 *Pie chart*

DELEGATE VIEWS ON TRAINER

Figure 6.7 *Line graph*

TRAINING EXPENDITURE/EMPLOYEE 1988–93

Figure 6.8 *Scatter diagram and regression line*

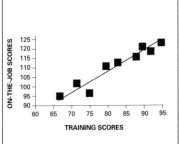

RELATIONSHIP BETWEEN ON-THE-JOB SCORES AND TRAINING SCORES

273

Numerical approaches

The most commonly used numerical methods for analysing evaluation data are:

- measures of location
- measures of dispersion
- scoring methods
- correlation and regression
- sampling and statistical inference
- significance testing.

All of these methods are well covered in the references at the end of the chapter, except scoring, so we will devote more space to that method than the others.

Measures of location

Measures of location are designed to give information about a certain part or location of the data. The most commonly used ones are measures of the central or middle location. These are:

- the mean or average – calculated by summing all the data items and dividing by the number of data items
- the median – the middle value of a set of data when it is arranged in numerical order, either from lowest to highest or vice versa
- the mode – the data value which occurs most frequently.

There are two other useful measures of location which provide a feel for the bottom half and the top half of the data respectively. These are related to the median and are:

- the lower quartile – the data value below which 25 per cent of the data items will fall and above which 75 per cent of the items occur (when the data is arranged in numerical order)
- the upper quartile – the value above which 25 per cent of the data items will occur and below which 75 per cent

of the data items will fall (when the data is arranged in numerical order).

Measures of dispersion

Measures of dispersion indicate how variable the data is. There are three measures of dispersion commonly used:

- the range – the difference between the lowest and highest value in the data set
- the inter-quartile range – the difference between the lower and upper quartile, ie the span of the middle 50 per cent of the data
- the standard deviation – a measure of the dispersion or spread of the data around the mean. The higher the standard deviation the more dispersed or variable the data.

Generally with evaluation results you are hoping for as little dispersion as possible. The less variable the data, the more focused the message.

Scoring methods

There is a range of scoring methods available. The two most common uses in evaluation are for:

- scoring semantic and Likert-type scales on questionnaires or observation forms;
- scoring before and after knowledge-based tests.

Example of a semantic differential scale. The question asked delegates to rate the trainer on a six-point scale.

	1	2	3	4	5	6	
Trainer has poor knowledge of area	1	2	3	4	5	6	Trainer has excellent knowledge of area
Results (nos of delegates)	2	3	3	4	2	1	15 delegates

The most commonly used method is to calculate an *average*.

$$\text{Average} = \frac{(2 \times 1) + (3 \times 2) + (3 \times 3) + (4 \times 4) + (2 \times 5) + (1 \times 6)}{15}$$

$$= \frac{49}{15}$$

$$= 3.3$$

An alternative method is to calculate the *score* as follows:

$$\text{Score} = \frac{(2 \times 1) + (3 \times 2) + (3 \times 3) + (4 \times 4) + (2 \times 5) + (1 \times 6)}{6 \times 15} \times 100$$

$$= \frac{49}{90} \times 100$$

$$= 54\%$$

Note: If the bottom end of the scale indicated a zero score, ie no knowledge, then it would be better to use a scale of zero to five.
   Both the above approaches assume that the intervals on the scale are perceived by the respondents as the same size.

Another popular approach is to express the results as a proportion or percentage of the total delegates.

The percentage of delegates that rated the trainer as 4, 5, or 6 $= \dfrac{7}{15} \times 100$

$$= 47\%$$

Example of a Likert type scale. The question asked delegates to tick the box which reflected their views on the quality of the catering on the training course

	Low quality	Fair quality	Good quality	Very good quality	
Nos of delegates	2	7	5	1	15 delegates

276

The most obvious approach here is to use percentages of the total number of delegates.

Percentage of delegates that rated the catering as of good or very good quality

$$= \frac{(5 + 1)}{15} \times 100$$

$$= 40\%$$

Alternatively, allocate a rating to each category, eg low quality = 1, fair quality = 2, etc. Then, use either an average or a score as below:

$$\text{Score} = \frac{(2 \times 1) + (7 \times 2) + (5 \times 3) + (1 \times 4)}{4 \times 15} \times 100$$

$$= \frac{35}{60} \times 100$$

$$= 58\%$$

The above approach has the advantage that it provides one figure that summarises the whole of the data, however again it is based on assuming that the respondents view the interval sizes as the same.

If the scale is clearly non-linear then reflect this in the allocating of the ratings. For example, delegates were rated as to their competency after training:

	Not meeting standard	Close to standard	Fully meets standard
No of delegates	2	5	8

Allocate a rating to each category, but consider a non-linear scale, eg not meeting standard = 1, close to standard = 4, fully meets standard = 5.

Score $= \dfrac{(2 \times 1) + (5 \times 4) + (8 \times 5)}{5 \times 15} \times 100$

$= \dfrac{62}{75} \times 100$

$= 83\%$

Example for scoring before and after knowledge-based tests.
Suppose a knowledge test consists of 20 questions and a
delegate scores 12 before the training and 16 after the training. Calculate a gain ratio to indicate the gain in learning.

Gain ratio $= \dfrac{\text{Post-test score} - \text{Pre-test score}}{\text{Possible score} - \text{Pre-test score}} \times 100$

$= \dfrac{16 - 12}{8} \times 100$

$= \dfrac{4}{8} \times 100$

$= 50\%$

The gain ratio for the whole course would be the average gain
ratio for all delegates. Alternatively the distribution of gain
ratios could be presented: eg, 60% of delegates achieved a
gain ratio of 50% or more, 20% achieved a gain ratio of
between 30% and 50%, and 20% achieved a gain ratio of less
than 30%.

Correlation and regression

Correlation measures the relationship between two sets of
data, often referred to as variables. Two sets of data or
variables are said to be correlated if changes in one are
accompanied by changes in the other. The variables are
positively correlated if they both move in the same direction,
eg as one increases so does the other. The variables are
negatively correlated if they move in opposite directions, eg
as one increases the other decreases. The strength of the

relationship is expressed in terms of the correlation co-efficient.

It is shown diagrammatically using a scatter diagram (see Figure 6.8 on page 273). This plots the results of the scores gained by delegates on a skill test held at the end of a training course, ie as part of the immediate evaluation of the course, with results of a skills test conducted back on the job, ie, as part of the intermediate evaluation of the course. Each point on the scatter diagram represents a delegate.

Using regression analysis, it is possible to fit a straight line to the data points which can then be used to make predictions (see Figure 6.8 on page 273). In the example given it would be possible to predict what the on-the-job score would be, based on the training score.

These techniques are useful for analyses such as:

- relating immediate evaluation results to intermediate results, ie evaluating the effectiveness of the immediate techniques for predicting performance back on the job
- for reliability testing, eg assessing whether self-assessment competency ratings made by delegates tallied with the assessments made by their managers.

Sampling and statistical inference

Often it is preferable to carry out an evaluation exercise on a sample, eg of delegates or of courses, rather than evaluate the complete population of delegates that have received training. Sampling has the advantages that it is usually a quicker and cheaper way of obtaining the required information. When the sample is chosen in a statistically correct way, valid con-clusions can be drawn about the larger population from the sample results. This process is called statistical inference. The sample will provide estimates of what the results would be if the whole population was surveyed and an important concern will be how good the estimate is, ie how close it is to the true value for the population. An important decision will be the size of the sample that needs to be taken. Deciding on the sample size and choosing a sample is not an easy task for the amateur. It is worth seeking advice from that friendly statistician!

Significance tests

Significance tests are used to test whether the results from one group are significantly different from another group, ie the differences are substantial enough that they could not be caused by chance variation. There is a range of significance tests available that are used in different circumstances.

These tests are useful for:

- comparing before and after training results
- comparing results with control group results
- comparing results between different trainers, training methods, etc.

Again this is quite a complex area. Choosing the appropriate test is important as is being very clear exactly what a significant result actually tells you. Try reading the relevant chapters of the books suggested at the end of this section or again seek advice!

Use of computers in evaluation

As discussed in the introduction to this chapter the advent of simple but sophisticated computer software has greatly increased the accessibility of analysis techniques to the Training Professional. There are three types of package that are potentially of most use. The first two are general packages, the third has been specially designed for training evaluation. These are:

- spreadsheet packages (such as Excel and Lotus) and also specialist statistical packages (such as SPSS) which can be used for quite sophisticated statistical analyses (eg calculating averages, standard deviations, correlation coefficients, carrying out regression analysis, significance tests) and preparing statistical charts (eg bar charts, histograms, graphs, pie charts)
- survey packages which are specifically designed for the preparation of questionnaires, their analysis and the presentation of results

- evaluation packages that have been specifically designed for the evaluation of training. These often form part of general training packages which include training needs analysis and training administration. Such packages generally take the form of providing simple questionnaires which can be modified and simple analyses such as calculating percentages and averages and presenting the information in the form of bar charts, pie charts and graphs. Most versions currently are directed at reaction level evaluation or simple recording of before and after competencies.

These last packages have the advantage that they are easy to use, but the disadvantage is that they often take a quite simplistic approach. The first two types of package are more powerful and more flexible, but require greater understanding of the techniques being used.

Further help

This chapter has aimed to provide an introduction and an overview of the various statistical techniques that can be employed to help analyse and present evaluation results. It is beyond the remit of this book to go into detail on the more complex approaches. There is a large number of books on the use and application of statistical techniques. For a gentle introduction to all the techniques try Bee & Bee (1990), while for a more in-depth read try Anderson, Sweeney and Williams (1987).

Conclusion

In this chapter we have covered briefly a range of analysis techniques. In summary, remember to:

- focus on the objectives of the evaluation study
- keep your analysis as simple as possible

281

- identify the messages you are getting from your analysis and then choose the best methods for conveying those messages.

Finally, don't be afraid to seek help — either from those friendly statisticians or by doing some further reading on areas of interest. In the next chapter we will look at what to do with all this information once you have got it.

24

Presenting and Using Evaluation Results

Introduction

We have planned and designed our study, collected the data and analysed the results. We are now at the crucial stage of presenting and using the evaluation information. The previous chapters have addressed the issues of evaluation in what could be described as an artificial environment − where evaluation is seen as scientific research into whether training is effective, where everyone takes an objective and unbiased view of the results of the process. In practice, as we all are well aware, the evaluation will be taking place in organisations where a number of factors may intervene to sully the scientific purity of the results or alter how the results are used. Evaluation, almost by definition, implies reviewing performance of individuals or groups of people, eg the training needs analyser, the training sponsor/initiator, the trainer, the delegates, the delegates' managers. Newby and Bramley (1984), in an interesting article, comment:

> Most evaluation feedback or research should be useful rather than threatening, but it can be argued that the training product can never be evaluated without also judging the trainer responsible.

They focus here on the trainer, probably because a lot of the evaluation that goes on focuses on the delivery. We would argue that the trainer is only one player, albeit an important one, in the training experience. However, it would be a very unusual organisation where the threat element is eliminated entirely. Also, although the articulated objective may be expressed in terms of assessing whether the training has met the business need, people may have their own agendas about what they want the evaluation process to achieve. Both these issues may affect the way in which people will participate in the evaluation process, either in terms of their willingness to be involved or in terms of whether they will consciously or subconsciously try to subvert the process.

Key issues

The process of evaluation is aided greatly if two key issues can be clarified at the outset:

- what the purpose of the evaluation study is
- who the client(s) is/are.

Again in terms of the purpose, there will usually be an overt aim, eg to establish whether the business need has been met, but there are sometimes covert ones as well, eg to look at the quality of the trainer, the support of the managers in the workplace, or even to prove whether evaluation itself is worthwhile. Since this whole book advocates the principle that the clearer the objectives, the more likely you will be to achieve them, it would be surprising if this did not apply to the evaluation process itself! The message here is if you are initiating and carrying out the evaluation study be clear what all your own objectives are, if you are the initiator bear in mind that the more you share your objectives with the executor of the study the more likely the evaluation study will be to meet them. If you are the executor an important first task may be to tease out all those objectives. Establishing who the client(s) are is not always straightforward either, eg is it the training manager or the sponsor of the training or both? If there is more than one client the issue of establishing the purpose of the study becomes more complex.

It is also important at the outset to consider, as far as is possible, how the results will be used and who will have access to the results. An ethical issue can occur when participants in an evaluation study have been told that their individual results will be regarded as confidential. It is vital at the planning stage to think through the implications of confidentiality and whether in fact it can be achieved.

Sometimes, it can prove difficult in practice and if this is the case it is far better not to suggest that it can.

It would also be naïve to suggest the way that evaluation studies are presented and then used will not be affected by organisational and political factors. It is rare that the evaluators themselves can be entirely objective because they will bring to the evaluation:

- some form of baggage in the way of preconceptions and assumptions. Sometimes this baggage will be useful and sometimes detrimental. The extent of the baggage will depend probably on the closeness of the relationship between the evaluator and those being evaluated.
- some level of concern about what the effects of an apparently critical evaluation will have on themselves, their part of the organisation, etc.

The outside evaluator, eg an external consultant, has the advantage and the disadvantage that preconceptions and assumptions are more limited. This may mean on the positive side that they do not go into the evaluation with any pre-conceived ideas about what the results of the study will show. On the downside they may be operating without an aware-ness of the values and concerns of those involved or of the organisation as a whole. When presenting the results it is a brave or foolhardy evaluator who will not think about what impact the findings will have on those who are involved and particularly on the clients and the recipients of the report. At a very obvious level, if one of the clients is the training manager to what extent may poor results from the study be seen as criticism of the training function or, if it is a line manager who sponsored or initiated the training, a reflection on the way they reached their decision to undertake the train-ing in the first place. Or even worse, what if it is a board initiative that turns out to be less than effective? An inside evaluator may feel inhibited by these pressures. An outside evaluator may be less affected but will also be aware that if the evaluation appears to be critical it may jeopardise the continuing relationship with the client!

Presenting evaluation results

There are no easy answers to these issues, the important point is the need to be aware of them. In presenting the evaluation results:

- focus on the objectives
- think about who the audience is – what information do they need, what will be the impact of the results?
- be clear about the strengths and weaknesses of the study in terms of methodology and the practicalities of data collection and analysis
- be constructive, eg highlighting areas for improvement rather than areas of weakness
- present the results in a professional way – writing a clear and succinct report, making good use of diagrammatic methods, etc
- be timely – agree an appropriate timescale for reporting at the outset of the study and then stick to it unless there are strong reasons for a change.

Using evaluation results

In using evaluation results:

- be aware of the impact of the results on those involved and decide on an appropriate strategy for addressing these issues and sensitivities
- decide who needs to see the results and in what form, eg detailed report to the sponsor, summary to the Board
- decide what consultation is required, with whom and on what, before deciding on what action is to be taken
- decide on appropriate action as quickly as possible and then take that action as quickly as is feasible
- feed the results back to those that have participated in the study, eg the delegates, their managers, the trainer

   – this will help sell the relevance of evaluation and motivate and encourage further participation.

Evaluation information is just like any other information — decisions made based on it will be affected by a whole range of factors and rightly so! However, this should not mean that what and how the results are acted upon relies on chance — how busy the training professional is at the time or how willing or *not* key players are to face up to some unpalatable issues. It is important, whatever decisions are taken, even where these may be not to follow up some of the proposals, to be clear on why these decisions have been taken.

Conclusion

In Section 6 we have sought to set out a structured approach to the evaluation of training programmes based on the traditional model of Kirkpatrick *et al*. This is essentially a goal-based approach and provides the basis for the strong link with the training needs analysis approach we have adopted. There are other approaches, eg 'goal-free evaluation' which is where the evaluator does not set off to measure success against particular objectives but to identify any changes achieved, 'responsive evaluation' which looks at the effects of a training programme in relation to the different stakeholders, and so on. We believe the traditional model of the four/five levels provides both a structured and a conceptually straightforward approach. This is important as the Training Professional will have to *sell* the need for and the benefits of evaluation to the delegates, his/her line colleagues, senior managers, etc.

There is often concern that evaluation will result in a plethora of forms, interviews, group discussions, which will swamp the unsuspecting delegates, their managers and just about anyone else who has been involved or shown an interest! There will also be concern that evaluation will be time consuming and expensive. The answer lies in keeping a sense of perspective. The most sophisticated evaluation studies should be reserved for the high-expenditure/high-profile programmes. Also, the Training Professional could decide to evaluate only a sample of programmes each year

and involve line colleagues in the choice of which programmes.

However, we hope that we have convinced you that under-
taking training evaluation is not only a vital and integral part
of the Training Wheel, but also that it is not such a daunting
challenge as it first appeared! Do not be afraid to tackle it in
easy stages and seek advice from your friendly line manager
colleagues, statisticians, finance professionals. Evaluation
should be a joint endeavour — the more people that are involved with the design and approach, the more *ownership* of
the results there will be and, most important of all, the
greater likelihood of appropriate action ensuing.

Section 7
Reflections

Reflections

In our introduction to this book we nailed our colours firmly to the mast in stating our view that the starting point for any training initiative must be the business needs of the organisation. We have gone on to say that the best way to meet those needs is to be systematic in researching who needs to be trained, in what areas, with what degree of priority, over what timescale and by what method(s). It is worth reflecting on the benefits of systematic TNA. These are that:

- training is targeted on the needs of the organisation
- training needs are identified in sufficient time to ensure they can be met in the most appropriate way
- it allows for prioritising to take place in a rational way
- it allows for budgets to be prepared in a rational way
- it enables training to be properly planned
- it enables training resources to be used efficiently and effectively
- it sets the foundation for the evaluation of the training
- it encourages ownership of the training by all those involved.

We have also introduced the concept of the Training Professionals as those who are trainers or are line managers seeing training as a part of their management responsibility in meeting business objectives. We have demonstrated the need for this professionalism in examining all solutions to the business needs analysis, not just the training option, and, once training is identified as the preferred option, the need to be very precise in defining what is required. We have stressed strongly that, when specifying the training that is required, the outcomes should be stated in measurable, behavioural terms in order to provide the foundation for training evaluation.

Finally, we have set out what we believe to be good

practice in training evaluation, at reaction, immediate, intermediate and ultimate levels, at all times linking back through the original TNA to the business needs. The benefits of training evaluation extend far beyond the direct and obvious ones of improving the quality of the training and ensuring the effectiveness of the training, to providing the basis for the training function and the Training Professional to be considered as serious members of the management team. By demonstrating that training delivers results, meets the business needs and represents a good investment of resources, the Training Professional will now be operating on the same, level playing field as their line and other professional colleagues.

In suggesting a systematic approach to meeting the business/training need we introduced the concept of the Training Wheel. However, we are aware that such a process is not always sequential in that it is sometimes not easy to categorise a particular activity as always preceding, or following, another given activity. In the real world certain activities, which for convenience of explanation we have kept separate, will be rolled up together.

We have also stressed in the book the necessity for the Training Professional to be concerned with the wider environment, to be familiar with the language of the accountant, the economist and the statistician, to be strategic in identifying the business needs and in meeting those needs. We recognise that we are not alone in making the case for the Training Professional to be proactive, rather than reactive, to what is going on in the organisation. In our reading of the literature we notice a ground swell towards a different role for the Training Professional — away from the role of provider of courses, to being the focal point of the learning organisation, with the training function (however it is managed) at the core of the organisation's business strategy.

We believe that many organisations have only scratched the surface of the full potential of training to take them forward into the future. This future, if nothing else, will be one where organisations will need to be more competitive and where survival and growth will depend on them being able to operate at optimum efficiency and effectiveness. It is a future where organisations will need to anticipate and respond to the ever-increasing pace of change and where the Training Professional can be at the forefront of meeting the business needs generated from these changes.

What a challenge for the Training Professional!

Bibliography

ANDERSON D, SWEENEY J and WILLIAMS T (1987). *Statistics for Business and Economics.* 3rd edn. West Publishing Co, St Paul

ANSOFF I (1987). *Corporate Strategy.* Rev edn. Penguin Books, Middlesex

ARMSTRONG M (1991). *A Handbook of Personnel Management Practice.* 4th edn. Kogan Page, London

BEE R and BEE F (1990). *Management Information Systems and Statistics.* IPM, London

BOAM R and SPARROW P (1992). *Designing and Achieving Competency: A competency approach to developing people and organisations.* McGraw-Hill, Maidenhead

BOYDELL T H (1990). *A Guide to the Identification of Training Needs.* 2nd edn. BACIE, London

CASCIO W F (1991). *Costing Human Resources: The financial impact of behaviour in organisations.* 3rd edn. PWS-Kent, Massachusetts

CLUTTERBUCK D (1991). *Everyone Needs a Mentor.* 2nd edn. IPM, London

COALEY K (1993). 'Financial Value and Management Training.' *Management Development Review.* Vol 6, No 2. pp 26–9

CONVERSE J M and PRESSER S (1986). *Survey Questions: Handcrafting the standardised questionnaire.* Sage Publications, London

DAVIES D (1990). *Finance and Accounting for Managers.* IPM, London

EMPLOYMENT DEPARTMENT (1991). *Investors in People – The National Standard, No 1.* Employment Department, Sheffield

EMPLOYMENT DEPARTMENT (1993). *Skills Needs in Britain.* Employment Department, Sheffield

FERDINAND R (1988). 'Management Training Needs Analysis (TNA).' *Industrial and Commercial Training.* Vol 20, No 5, September/October. pp 27–31

GOLDSTEIN I L (1986). *Training in Organisations: Needs assessment, development and evaluation.* 2nd edn. Brooks/Cole Publishing Company, California

HAMBLIN A C (1974). *Evaluation and Control of Training.* McGraw-Hill, Maidenhead

HANDY C (1989). *The Age of Unreason.* Business Books Ltd, London

HERBERT G R and DOVERSPIKE D (1990). 'Performance Appraisal in the Training Needs Analysis Process: A review and critique.' *Public Personnel Management.* Vol 19, No 3, Fall. pp 253–70

HICKS O J Jr (1990). *Information Systems in Business: An introduction.* 2nd edn. West Publishing Co, St Paul

JACKSON T (1989). *Evaluation: Relating training to business performance.* Kogan Page, London

JOHNSON G and SCHOLES K (1993). *Exploring Corporate Strategy: Text and cases.* 3rd edn. Prentice-Hall, London

KIRKPATRICK D L (1967). 'Evaluation of Training.' In CRAIG R L and BITTEL L R (eds), *Training and Evaluation Handbook.* McGraw-Hill, New York

KUBR M and PROKOPENKO J (1989). *Diagnosing Management Training and Development Needs: Concept and techniques.* ILO, Geneva

KURAITIS V P (1981). 'The Personnel Audit.' *Personnel Administrator.* Vol 26, Part II

LUCEY T (1991). *Management Information Systems.* 6th edn. DP Publications Ltd, London

MAGER R F (1991a). *Goal Analysis.* 2nd edn. Kogan Page, London

MAGER R F (1991b). *Measuring Instructional Results.* 2nd edn. Kogan Page, London

MAGER R F (1991c). *Preparing Instructional Objectives.* 2nd edn. Kogan Page, London

MAGER R F and PIPE P (1991). *Analysing Performance Problems.* 2nd edn. Kogan Page, London

'Management Training "Saves Millions".' *Personnel Management Plus.* Vol 5, No 1, January 1994. p 6

MANPOWER SERVICES COMMISSION (1981). *Glossary of Training Terms.* 3rd edn. HMSO, London

NEWBY A C (1992). *Training Evaluation Handbook*. Gower, Aldershot

NEWBY A C and BRAMLEY P (1984). 'The Evaluation of Training Part II: The organisational context.' *Journal of European Industrial Training*. Vol 8, No 7

OLIVAS L (1983). 'Designing and Conducting a Training Needs Analysis: Putting the horse before the cart.' *Journal of Management Development*. Vol 2, No 4

OPPENHEIM A N (1992). *Questionnaire Design, Interviewing and Attitude Measurement*. 2nd edn. Pinter, London

PEARN M and KANDOLA R (1993). *Job Analysis: A manager's guide*. 2nd edn. IPM, London

RANDELL G A, PACKARD P M A, SHAW R L and SLATER A J (1984). *Staff Appraisal: A first step to effective leadership*. 3rd edn. IPM, London

REGALBUTO G A (1992). 'Targeting the Bottom Line.' *Training and Development*. Vol 46, No 4, April. pp 29–32

ROBBINS S P (1988). *Management: Concepts and applications*. 2nd edn. Prentice-Hall, New Jersey

ROBINSON D G and ROBINSON J C (1989). *Training for Impact*. Jossey-Bass, San Francisco

SENGE P (1990). *The Fifth Discipline: The art and practice of the learning organisation*. Doubleday, New York

SLOMAN M (1993). 'Training to Play a Lead Role.' *Personnel Management*. Vol 25, No 7, July. pp 40–42

SLOMAN M (1994). 'Coming in From the Cold: A new role for trainers.' *Personnel Management*. Vol 26, No 1, January. pp 24–7

SMITH B and DELAHEYE B (1988). 'Training Needs Analysis: A marketing viewpoint.' *Journal of European Industrial Training*. Vol 12, No 2

STEADMAN S V (1980). 'Learning to Select a Needs Assessment Strategy.' *Training and Development Journal*. No 30, January, pp 56–61. Reported in GOLDSTEIN I L (1986), *Training in Organisations: Needs assessment, development and evaluation*. 2nd edn. Brooks/Cole Publishing Co, California

STEWART V and STEWART A (1978). *Managing the Manager's Growth*. Gower, Farnborough

STEWART V, STEWART A and FONDA N (1981). *Business*

Applications of Repertory Grid. McGraw-Hill, Maidenhead

TANNENBAUM R and SCHMIDT W (1958). 'How to Choose a Leadership Pattern.' *Harvard Business Review.* March-April

THARENOU P (1991). 'Managers Training Needs and Preferred Training Strategies.' *Journal of Management Development.* Vol 10, No 5. pp 46–59

TRAINING AGENCY (1989). *Training in Britain.* HMSO, London

Transport and Works Act 1992. HMSO, London.

TYSON S and JACKSON T (1992). *The Essence of Organisational Behaviour.* Prentice-Hall, London

WALLUM P (1993). 'A Broader View of Succession Planning.' *Personnnel Management.* Vol 25, No 9, September. pp 42–5

WARR P, BIRD M and RACKHAM N (1970). *Evaluation of Management Training.* Gower Press, London

WHITELAW M (1972). *The Evaluation of Management Training – A preview.* IPM, London

WOODRUFFE C (1990). *Assessment Centres: Identifying and developing competence.* IPM, London

WOODRUFFE C (1992). 'What is Meant by a Competency?' In BOAM R and SPARROW P (eds), *Designing and Achieving Competency: A competency-based approach to developing people and organisations.* McGraw-Hill, Maidenhead

YOUNG T L (1993). *Planning Projects: 20 steps to effective project planning.* Industrial Society, London

Index

Other titles available from the IPD

Tools for Assessment and Development Centres
Pearn Kandola

This is a comprehensive set of accessible, practical and leading-edge tools for organisations that want to introduce assessment or development centres, or to measure the effectiveness of existing centres. The toolkit is the result of extensive research in the field by Pearn Kandola, working with top UK companies, and all the tools have been reviewed and tested by experienced designers and users. The material is presented as five units (four ringbinders and one spiral-bound book) in a polypropylene briefcase:

1 Overview (spiral-bound book, 32 pages) − a succinct introduction to the chain-link model, the development of the tools, practical guidance on using the pack, and further reference sources.

2 Tools for defining criteria/competencies for centres (ringbinder, 88 pages) − 11 tools to guide managers to defining criteria that relate the needs of the organisation to the demands of current job roles.

3 Tools for designing assessment exercises (ringbinder, 96 pages) − seven stages in exercise design are described, supported with 12 tools to make the task easier and ensure that exercises are appropriate and fair.

4 Tools for preparing people (ringbinder, 128 pages) − this section is divided into two parts: seven tools on preparing assessors and another seven on preparing participants and managers.

5 Tools for auditing centres (ringbinder, 88 pages) − nine tools provide the key steps to ensuring that centres make a meaningful and worthwhile contribution to individual and organisational goals.

1996   ISBN 0 85292 631 6   **£500.00**

Tools for a Learning Organisation
Pearn Kandola

The only organisations to survive in the future will be learning organisations. These organisations continuously transform themselves – they harness and develop everyone's potential by creating a learning culture to ensure the release of talent. *Tools for a Learning Organisation* is the first practical aid to turn theory into reality. All the tools in the pack have been rigorously tested and evaluated. The pack contains four units (two A4 spiral-bound books and two A4 ringbinders) in a polypropylene briefcase:

1 Introduction (spiral-bound book, 40 pages) – a summary of the key issues, with practical guidance on using the pack and further reference sources.

2 Workshop Plans (spiral-bound book, 38 pages) – each workshop plays an important role in the five different, but linked, ways of getting started – Gaining Commitment, Auditing Learning in the Organisation, Planning and Implementation, Helping Managers to Manage Learning, and Reviewing the Role of Training and Trainers.

3 Exercises (ringbinder, 360 pages) – over 30 practical exercises to analyse learning, enhance learning skills and support individual and team learning. The exercises can be pursued in the five workshops, or used on a stand-alone basis.

4 Instruments (ringbinder, 120 pages) – well-documented support material that includes The Learning Climate, Learning Blockages, and Job Learning Analysis Questionnaires.

Striving to become a learning organisation with the aid of these tools will help organisations seeking accreditation as Investors in People. Cross-references are made where relevant to IIP assessment indicators, MCI competencies and NVQ/SVQ levels.

Second Edition   1995   ISBN 0 85292 593 X   **£400.00**

New Training Series from the IPD

Management Shapers is a comprehensive series covering all the crucial management skill areas. Each book includes the key issues, helpful starting-points and practical advice in a concise and lively style. Together they form an accessible library reflecting current best practice – ideal for study or quick reference.

The Appraisal Discussion
Terry Gillen

The Disciplinary Interview
Alan Fowler

Effective Learning
Alan Mumford

Leadership Skills
John Adair

Listening Skills
Ian MacKay

Making Meetings Work
Patrick Forsyth

Managing Your Time
Iain Maitland

Negotiating, Persuading and Influencing
Alan Fowler

The Selection Interview
Penny Hackett

Working in Teams
Alison Hardingham